ALL THE MOMMIES
WOULD GO PAINTING
TOGETHER

BY ALICE L. GERBER

ALL RIGHTS RESERVED
April 11, 2013
Copyright Applied

ISBN: 978-0-615-80153-7

Book cover designed by Susanne L. Gerber

Book printed by

Brune Printing Company

310 W. Perry St. • Paulding, OH 45879
www.bruneprinting.com

Permission from several businesses was obtained in order to complete this story. This includes reprinting of various news clippings, news photographs, obituaries and advertisements. The businesses are:
Paulding County Carnegie Library, Susan Pieper, Director (Paulding, Ohio)
Paulding Progress Newspaper, Melinda Huseby Krick, Editor (Paulding, Ohio)
Defiance Cresent News, Steve VanDemark, General Manager (Defiance, Ohio)
The Toledo Blade Newspaper, Luann Sharp, Editor (Toledo, Ohio)
The permission statements are highlighted per the appropriate reprinted articles, documents, advertisements, photographs, and/or obituaries.

There is no explanation for this book. It is something that I simply had to do. I just had to do this....

So everybody, get your **ART** on!
Here we go, celebrating our mommies, our daddies who got their ART on!
Everybody get your he**ART** on!

This book is dedicated to all of our mothers who found such release and joy in the painting of our towns, and landscapes. This book is written for the mothers with whom I was aware my mother spent time. Please know that there were likely others of whom I was not aware, and no forethought was intended for any to be missed. While not represented within this book, many created works in the arenas of charcoal, china, ceramics, and tole painting.

I graciously thank those mothers who agreed to be interviewed for this project ~ as well as one dad, Gene Scarbrough, who continues to contribute to the delinquency of art regularly. This assisted in capturing your stories, your great works, and your friendships. I send an acclamation out to my two daughters, Audra and Susanne, who have always been my constants in my life, and to Ron Johnson who has been by my side. This acclamation also goes to my brothers who participated in an interview regarding our mother.

A compassionate thank you to those participating in my search for pictures and history involved in creating this book. *Cheers go out to Lennie and Kathie (Clark) Roth, Connie (Clark) Waters, Barbara (Rife) Koch, Mayor Greg White, Rose Mary (Noneman) Carnahan, Keri (Noneman) Erne, Melissa (Peeper) Munger, Lynda (Englehart) Ringler, Rowena & Bill Bashore, all of the Paulding Co Library staff, & Melinda Huseby Krick.* A thank you to the <u>Paulding Progress</u>, the <u>Defiance Crescent</u> and the <u>Toledo Blade</u> for granting permission to reprint articles, photos, advertisements and/or obituaries. Without their total attentiveness, support and guidance this quest would not have made it to print.

Through each of you, this book became complete. Kudos to all!

God knew what He was doing, when He instilled within each of our mothers' hearts the curiosity, joy and bond that this endowment created.

Thank you for the selfless service of our men and women veterans. You have kept America safe, secure and free! Thank you to any new servicemen and women who currently are protecting us!

Mothers paint our lives in such grand ways.
They fill us up with all the colors of the world.

May you see your mother's colors everywhere.
God bless you and your family.
Sincerely,
~al!ce g

Table of Contents

The Wall That Started it All
The Instant Poem
One Year Later - A Celebration Party
Our Mommies Activities, Travels, Art Shows
The Interviews
 The Mommies Would Go Painting
 The Daddies, the Menfolk
The Eulogy Tributes
Epilogue

THE WALL THAT STARTED IT ALL:

From the top to right : *Wall Street Market*~ watercolor by Fern White ; *Ice Skating* ~watercolor by Dr Edna Preston; *"Weible" Barn*~ oil by Dr E C Pritchard ; *Sugar Beet*~ oil by Dr E C Pritchard; and *Depot*~ watercolor by Dr Edna Preston.
That is Mom's paint brush attached to the wall. Within seconds of these paintings being anchored onto the wall, a poem emitted from my heart.

The instant poem : <u>All the Mommies Would Go Painting Together</u>

 11-02-07

This weekend
I brought my mom
to a new gallery.
I have her abililty
displayed throughout
my home.
Included works are also some of
her best friends.
There is one wall, small,
that portrays my
hometown,
when I was very small.
My mommy feels closer now
& I believe is feeling happy
for her new site.

✏All the mommies would go ✏
painting together.
Each sat @ a different angle
yet displayed the same
subject
subjectively.
Yes all the mommies would go
painting together.
How they raised their brushes
and us
at the same time
speaks well of their souls.
Mrs **Guingrich** likely was the steward
in charge of all of us lads & lasses.

I see my history again,
items that are no longer there.
I smile seeing my hometown again
created by the hands of
all of the mommies
who would go painting together.

Our mommies were proof that
oil and water do mix!   * ~al!ce pritchard gerber

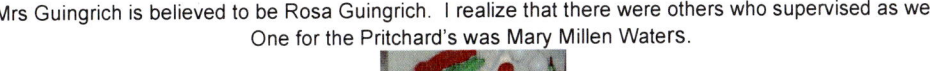

Mrs Guingrich is believed to be Rosa Guingrich. I realize that there were others who supervised as well.
One for the Pritchard's was Mary Millen Waters.

Almost one year later……. Invitation, Party and pictures…………….

Life is moving way too fast and I am having trouble keeping up with a lot of things that are important to me. I have talked for some time of having the Mommies come out to share in the history of their escapades of painting etc. And the summer is already gone………!

I have paintings that have been framed, reframed, some that have not been seen for a while. While this is short notice, I am hoping that you will be able to come by for a lookseee, to reminisce and share any of the paintings that you may want to bring along to show as well.

Please keep in mind that I am a Pritchard still but do my best not to have tooo many magazines about or dust bunnies either. However I am sure my lack of housekeeping will still show, so please just look past it all. ☺

On Saturday, October 11 you are cordially invited to my house for some refreshing drinks and sugary items to munch on-but nothing substantial to eat, just so you know! This will run from noon to 4:00! And you can come and go as you please, or have the time. Hope to see you then.

I want to thank all of the Mommies at this time too for being involved with our childhood, practicing group or block parenting and !!!! just taking the time to care for all of us whom you touched.

All the Mommies would go
Painting . . .
Saturday October 11
Noon to 4:00pm
@
10991 SR 111
Paulding, Ohio
*
419-399-4369
Unlisted

(2008)

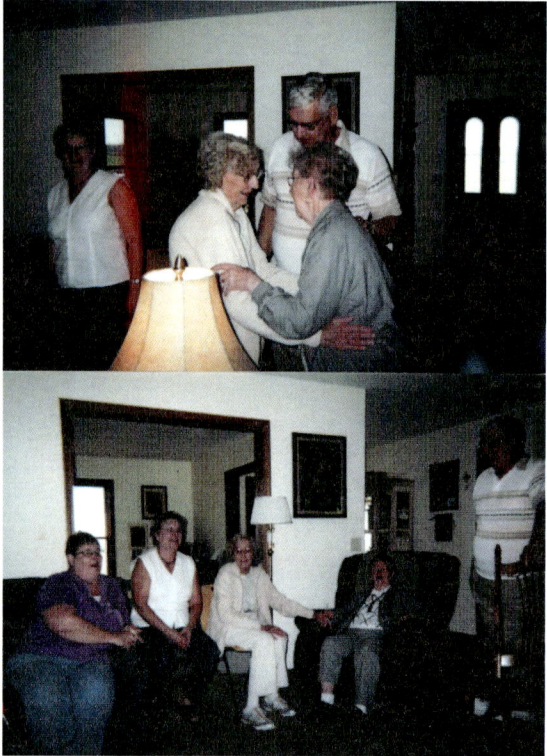

Gail Choate Maybee / Mary Millen Waters /Vine and Tiny Choate
Rhoda Choate Lewis /Gai l/Mary /Tiny and Vine

Marilyn Buehler and Becky Fishbaugh
Marilyn and Marie Moore

Choates and me
Mary and me

Buzz Carnahan / me / Mable Seslar

Proof that they did indeed paint the same subject. Isabelle's is in water color and obviously at the same post!

Tiny Vine and Mabel Seslar   Mary Ruth Clark and Deloris Whirrett

Ruth Gerber /Eileen Vance Jeffery /Sue Wilhelm   Isabelle Ringler /Buzz Carnahan /Ruth Gerber
Dr Larry Fishbaugh and Jack Moore   Vicki Carnahan Kadesh / Jack / Isabelle

Our Mommies Activities, Travels, Art Shows

Our Mommies Activities, Travels, Art Shows

*A more complete listing of participating artists found via newspaper documents list would *add* :
Antwerp : Jean Hughes; Mary Marlin; Mary Schilb; Mrs Richard Schilb and Mrs Verne Tussing
Oakwood/Defiance & 5 Span area : Verde Leatherman; Charles Leatherman; Chester Leatherman; Jean Dunlap and Martha McCague
Paulding: Olive Johnson, Mrs John Schaefer (Dr Schaefer who went into missions); Peg Dotterer: Joyce Huseby; Nancy Stiger; Millie Zug: Wilma Miller; and Barbara Zimmer
Et al Paulding Co names : Ester Corwin; Joy Deken; Myra Tow; Sylvia Young; and Bob Lindsay.
Please know that this is likely an incomplete listing of the total individuals who were our county's artists. This is compiled from what I could find.

Joyce Huseby and daughter Melinda Huseby Krick

✒Articles from historical consolidated Paulding Democrat and Paulding Republican county newspapers, which evolved into the Paulding Progress, begin here. Paulding Progress/Melinda Huseby Krick, Editor, has granted permission to reprint the articles regarding local artists of the 1950s and 1960s. Payne Reflector was bought by the Progress,which granted permission to reprint the Payne clipping. March 11, 2013
✒Article from Defiance Crescent newspaper of 1956 is reprinted with permission from the Defiance Crescent News/Steve VanDemark, General Manager. March 11, 2013
✒Oakwood newspaper no longer exist.
📖Paulding County Carnegie Library activities : Items from the Library's scrapbook of memories, copied with Permission from the Paulding County Carnegie Library, Susan Pieper. March 11, 2013

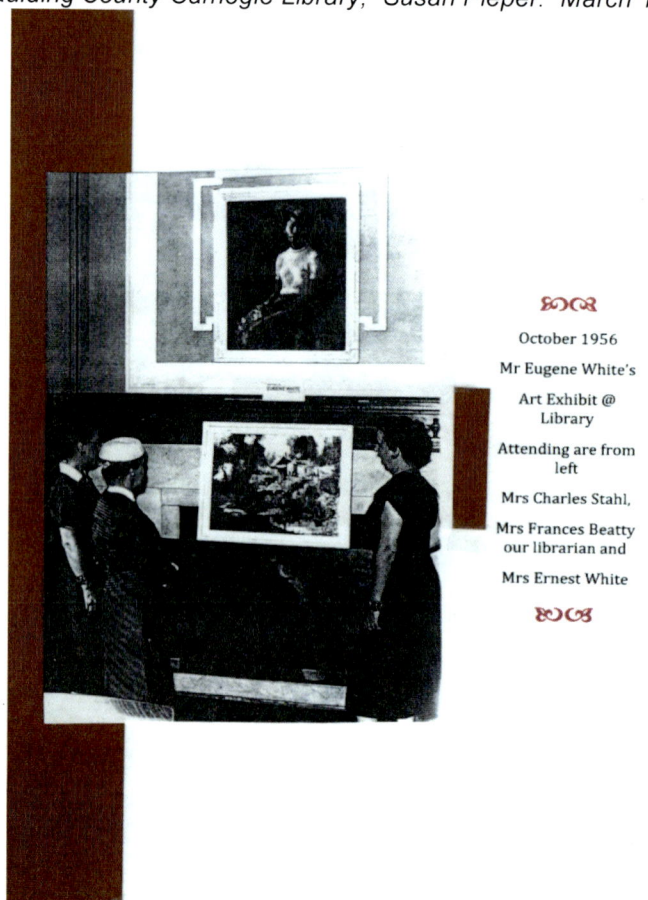

ℬ◯ℛ

October 1956

Mr Eugene White's

Art Exhibit @ Library

Attending are from left

Mrs Charles Stahl,

Mrs Frances Beatty our librarian and

Mrs Ernest White

ℬ◯ℛ

Library Scrapbook

Flower Show Ceramic And Painting Exhibit

1956

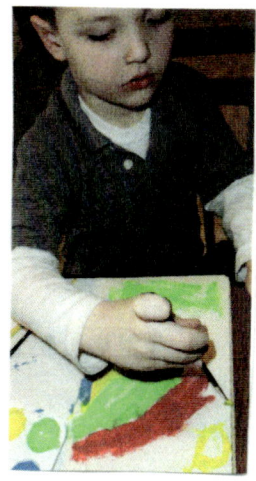

Showing To Be Held Thurs. & Fri. In The Paulding Library

Flowers, ceramics and paintings will be the theme for the Annual Flower Show to be held June 7th and 8th in the Library Basement. The time 7 until 9 P. M. on Thursday and 2-5, 7-9 P. M. on Friday.

Anyone wishing to bring cut flowers, house plants of any type, or specimens (a single flower) are cordially invited to bring them to the Library between 10-12 A. M. on Thursday.

Mrs. Cleon White of Van Wert will judge the arrangements Thursday afternoon, but again we wish to stress for those who would like to bring flowers for display only, we shall have a miscellaneous table.

June 7

Exhibit Shown In Paulding

PAULDING—The art exhibit of paintings by Mrs. Fern White and Mrs. Katherine Stahl is being held over another week and will be open to the public Saturday from 2 to 5 and 7 to 9 p.m. in the Paulding County Library.

The exhibits were held last week in conjunction with the Paulding Better Homes and Gardens Club Flower Show.

Both of the artists have exhibited in various shows, the latest one being in Montpelier last September.

Mrs. White entered a black and white oil painting of Mac-o-chee Castle in the Ohioana Library annual competition, and one of Mrs. Stahl's still-lifes was accepted for showing at the Fort Wayne Area Artists Exhibit.

Both women have studied under Lawrence Van Porth, director of the Florida Academy of Art at Tampa, Fla.; Prof. Harry Carnahan of Columbia University, and Eugene White of Sarasota, Fla. They are members of the Amateur Artists Association of America, the Lima Art Association and the Montpelier Artist's Club.

Defiance June 12

Art Exhibit At Paulding Saturday

Due to the many requests, the Art Exhibit by Mrs. Fern White and Mrs. Katherine Stahl, which was held last week in conjunction with the Better Homes and Gardens Club Flower Show at the Paulding Library, will be held over another week and will be open to the public on Saturday, June 16th from 2 to 5 in the afternoon and from 7 to 9 p. m.

Mrs. White and Mrs. Stahl have both studied under Lawrence Von Porth, Director of the Florida Academy of Arts at Tampa, Fla.; Prof. Harry Carnahan, of Columbia University and are just beginning a series of lessons under the direction of Mr Eugene White of Sarasota, Fla., and Middlepoint, Ohio. The women are also members of the Amateur Artists Ass'n., of America; The Lima Art Ass'n, and the Montpelier Artist's' Club.

Oakwood June 14

PAULDING—The art exhibit of paintings by Mrs. Fern White and Mrs. Katherine Stahl, which was held last week in conjunction with the Better Homes and Gardens Club Flower Show at the Paulding County Library, will be held over another week and will be open to the public on Saturday, June 16th, from 2 to 5 in the afternoon, and from 7 to 9 P. M.

The paintings of Mrs. Stahl and Mrs. White are becoming increasingly well-known throughout northwest Ohio and Indiana. Both of the women have exhibited in various shows, a recent one being in Montpelier in September. A black and white oil painting of Mac-o-chee Castle was entered in the Ohioan Library annual competition by Mrs. White while Mrs. Stahl has a still life showing a slice of watermelon, cantaloupe and peaches, accepted for the Fort Wayne Area Artists Show.

Mrs. White and Mrs. Stahl have both studied under Mr. Lawrence Van Porth, Director of the Florida Academy of Art at Tampa, Florida; Professor Harry Carnahan, of Columbia University and are just beginning a series of lessons under the direction of Mr. Eugene White, of Sarasota, Florida, and Middlepoint, Ohio. The women are also members of The Amateur Artists Association of America, The Lima Art Association and The Montpelier Artist's Club.

No one should miss seeing this interesting and worthwhile exhibit. If you are like the writer you will want to pick out your favorite painting and then go to see it again and again. Mrs. White is showing a recently painted still life entitled Mother's Day that is outstanding in design and color. A modern "ink resist" composition in an entirely different vein is also of great interest. Being an old Floridian, the writer has a case of acute nostaglia when she views "The Bait Shack" which was painted by Mrs. Stahl when she was in Bradenton, and which captures the very essence and feeling of Florida, "Our Dock on the Auglaize" is equally outstanding.

But - you will want to visit the exhibit and select your own favorites. Don't forget - Saturday night from 7 to 9 o'clock and Saturday afternoon from 2 to 5 in the clubroom of the Paulding County Library.

Payne June 14

Library Scrapbook

Continuing 1957 and 1958

Outstanding Art Exhibit At Paulding Library

The exhibit of fifty paintings by fifty contemporary American artists which opened at the Paulding County Library last Thursday is attracting an unusually large number of visitors, it was announced by Mrs. Frances F. Beatty, librarian. The exhibit is of a professional nature such as is usually only seen in museums in the larger cities and it is a rare privilege for Paulding and for the library to be able to show it.

The showing is being sponsored by the Paulding County Library and by the Paulding Artists Association. The paintings may be seen during regular library hours from 12:00 to 8:30 P.M. Members of the Artists Association are acting as hostesses.

The paintings which comprise the exhibition are extremely varied and depict regions of the United States from Maine to California. Techniques range from the purest transparent watercolor to gouache, casein and tempera with one oil for contrast. The showing has come to Paulding through the courtesy of the Ford Motor Company as a cultural and educational service to the community.

One of the unusual paintings in the collection is Lobster Festival, by F. Wenderoth Sanders. "For three days a year, the waterfront at Rockland, Maine becomes a carnival for lobster-lovers. Here Mr. Sanders pictures the crowd and the harbor where the real business of the festival-eating takes place." Another is Hotel del Coronado, California, which delightfully depicts a resort hotel in a semi-tropical park. It is by George Post. Still another, nostalgic in nature, is Haying Time, by Charles B. Allerton, a man in his eighties.

Members of Artist Association, who are serving as hostesses are: Mrs. Glenn Wythe, Mrs. Charles Stahl, Mrs. Julia Pope, Mrs. Olive Johnson, Mrs. Ernest White, Mrs. Paul R. Ringler, Mrs. Toria Leslie and Mrs. Helen Harrod.

Arrangements for the exhibit have been made by Mrs. Charles Stahl, Mrs. Ernest White, Rev. William Stewart and Mrs. Beatty.

Paulding January 31

The first county-wide art show for Paulding County painters held in the reading rooms of the Paulding County Library. Sponsor of the exhibition, the Paulding Art Association, was pleased at the response of both artists and the public to the showing. Eighty-six paintings, water colors and drawings are on display, from the brushes of 26 local artists. Five men were among the artists contributing. Besides Paulding artists there were contributions from Antwerp, Oakwood, and Cecil.

The Paulding Art Association is finding the greatest response to its work in the several years it existed. Its 24 members have been very busy this past winter, many of them joining in painting sessions on both the Wednesday night club meeting and the Saturday afternoon sessions with n Nartker of Kalida as instructor. Mrs. Robert Vance is president of the Association; Mrs. Alva bb, vice-president; and Dr. Edythe Pritchard has served as chairman of the show, which will come close next week, May 7th.

As a result of the wide public response to the several art exhibitions during the past year in Library, the Library Board is in the process now of installing special lighting for future shows. In the photo, left to right, are: Mrs. Alva Webb, vice-pres. of the Association, Mrs. Frank None-l, member and exhibitor, Mrs. Robert Vance, president of Association.

May 1

End of Library Scrapbook

1960

PAULDING PROGRESS THURSDAY FEB. 18, 1960

Paulding Woman's Club Entertains At Guest Nite

Dr. John Klassen demonstrates making pottery to members of Paulding Woman's Club.

The Paulding Woman's Club entertained with their annual guest night party Monday evening, February 15, in the club rooms at the Library.

The president, Mrs. Glenn Gallagher welcomed the guests and members. Mrs. Ernest Burnett introduced several young people who entertained with musical selections. Judy Boundy and Carol Fisher presented piano solos, Sue Smith a vocal solo and Jay Gillett a trombone solo.

Mrs. Burnett then presented the speaker Dr. John Klassen, a retired art teacher in Bluffton College, Bluffton, Ohio. Mr. Klassen is a man of unique background and experience and has this to say about himself -

"I was born and raised in Ukraine, Russia. We were Dutch people. In 1786, Catherine the Great had invited our forefathers to come to Russia, serve as model farmers, and teach the Russian people the basic principles of practical and sound agriculture. This our people did for five generations. We soon transformed what used to be a wilderness into a blooming garden and made Ukraine the breadbasket of Russia. The Russian Revolution eliminated free and independent farming. Consequently, since 1923, our people began to migrate to Canada and South America.

I came with my wife and one child to Bluffton, Ohio and was employed as an art teacher in Bluffton College. In Bluffton I have spent the last 36 years. I received my education in Basil, Switzerland and my art training in Munich, Germany. Before we came to America I was teaching art in a teacher-training school in Russia. In 1945 I was awarded the Ralph H. Beaton Memorial Prize in sculpture at the Columbus Gallery of Fine Arts. For seven summers I have worked as a craft instructor in summer camps for the University of Illinois."

Mr. Klassen's subject, 'The Spiritual Meaning of the Potter's Wheel,' was a demonstration of the making of a beautiful pitcher from a ball of white clay and likened to the spiritual life of man.

Following the program refreshments were served with Iris Gallagher and Olive Johnson presiding at the table which was beautifully decorated in a red and white Valentine theme.

Guests and members who enjoyed the evening were: Miss Evelyn Allshouse, Mrs. Ernest Burnett, Mrs. Harold Boundy, Mrs. Charles Clark, Mrs. Mitchell Boundy, Mrs. Bernard Dangler, Mrs. Rolland Fisher, Miss Roma Frey, Mrs. Glen Gallagher, Mrs. Owen Stuart, Miss Catherine Geyer, Miss Ruby Voke, Mrs. John Geyer, Mrs. Iris Kurs, Mrs. Harold Wood, Mrs. Dorr Elick, Mrs. Norman Gordon, Mrs. Kenneth Greer, Mrs. Herbert Monroe, Mrs. Olive Johnson, Mrs. Ernest White, Miss Flossie Kenny, Mrs. Robert Medaugh, Mrs. Bernard Seslar, Miss Joy Munger, Mrs. Herald Yenser, Mrs. Lloyd Parson, Mrs. Paul Spriggs, Mrs. John Peepers, Mrs. Isaac Thomas, Mrs. Charles Barson, Mrs. Roy Point, Mrs. Henry Brune, Mrs. R. S. Wheeler, Mrs. John Swartout, Mrs. Homer Zimmer, Mrs. Marcus Ptak, Mrs. Genevieve Keysor, Mrs. Wilmer Rekeweg, Mrs. Frank Morisy, Miss Lucile Russell, Mrs. Henry Smith, Mrs. Floyd Simons, Mrs. Rhoda Fox, Mrs. James Beattie, Mrs. Edna Preston, Mrs. DeNellda Schall, Mrs. Paul Herbst, Mrs. Paul Leidel, Mrs. Harvey Hyman, Mrs. Charles Stahl, Mrs. Kirkwood Pritchard, Mrs. Robert Vance, Mrs. Frank Noneman, Mrs. Paul Ringler, Mrs. Albert Rife, Mrs. Miriam Smith, Mrs. Bill Weible, Mrs. George Simon, Mrs. Herbert Meek, Mrs. Lelia Mouser, Mrs. John Schaefer and Dr. and Mrs. John Klaussen.

Spring Is On The Way!

SEE LIVE MODELS WEARING THE

'dated Paper Of The Paulding Democrat and Paulding Co. Republican

PAULDING, OHIO THURSDAY, MAY 25, 1961

PAULDING ARTISTS TO EXHIBIT IN FORT WAYNE SHOW

It has been announced that the Ft Wayne Artist's Guild in cooperation with the Downtown Businessman's Association will hold an Outdoor Art Exhibition on the Court House Square Saturday May 27th. The one day exhibit will give the Court House Square the atmosphere of the Paris Left Bank as artists and interested spectators mingle to enjoy the Free Exhibition. May 27th has been declared Ft Wayne Fine Arts Day and the Public is cordially invited to the Show where Paintings, Sculpture and Demonstartion will be featured.

Kate Stahl and Ferneau White of Paulding will have paintings in the Exhibit.

05.25.1961

Paulding Artists To Exhibit In Ft. Wayne Show

It has been announced that the Ft. Wayne Artist's Guild in Cooperation with the Downtown Businessmen's Association will hold an Outdoor Art Exhibition on the Court House Square Saturday, May 27th. The one day exhibit will give the Court House Square the atmosphere of the Paris Left Bank as artists and interested spectators mingle to enjoy the Free Exhibition. May 27th has been declared Ft. Wayne Fine Arts Day, and the public is cordially invited to the show where Paintings, Sculpture and Demonstrations will be featured.

Kate Stahl and Ferneau White of Paulding will have paintings in the Exhibit.

...L FIND IT IN THE W...

...SERVICE • EMPLOYMEN...

...sifieds on Page 8

Dr. Edna Preston, Chiropodist will be in her office at 342 S. Williams St. to care for patients after July 12. 37c1

WHEN YOU SE... the best SERVIC... NET CHECK... and oats to... the best tr... storage... rail ar... you... at...

STANLEY PRODUCTS can be ... in ... 35c3

07-13-61

IN YOUR CHAIN SAW FOR A MIGHTY NEW McCULLOCH

AN ALL-NEW McCULLOCH COSTS AS LITTLE AS $124.95

WERLING'S FURNITURE & APPLIANCE STORE Paulding, Ohio

FOR SALE

FOR RENT

CHRISTMAS TREES ON SALE BY SENIOR CLASS OF PAULDING AT THE POLAR CONE LARGE SELECTION

"LET GEORGE DO IT" APPLIANCE REPAIR

FREE TURKEY WITH THE PURCHASE OF $15 OR MORE IN FURNITURE, OR ANY MAJOR APPLIANCE

CASSEL'S Hardware • Furniture • Jewelry PAULDING, OHIO

REAL HUNGRY DAILY SPECIALS 75c JOHNSON'S

REAL ESTATE FOR SALE

FARMS FOR SALE

RIGGENBACH BROS. BUILDERS

ATTENTION FARMERS AND TRUCKERS

MEADOWBROOK COAL CO.

GLENN W. BAIR Realtor and Auctioneer

Snodgrass Poultry House

Paulding Grain And Seed, Inc.

GORRELL BROS. REAL ESTATE

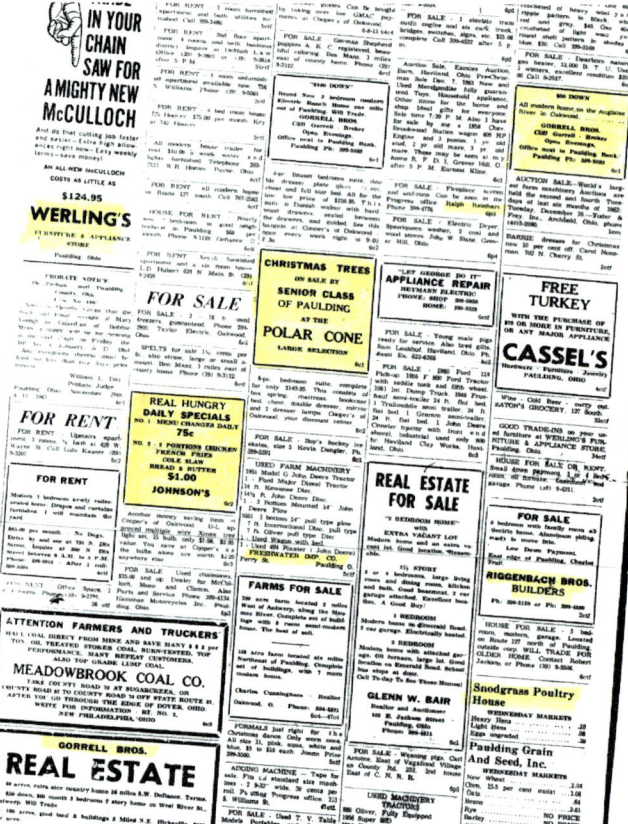

PAINT TOGETHER SESIONS START MARCH 14

The art Class is planning a few Wednesday eventings, "Paint Together" sessions at the Paulding County Library starting March 14 @ 7:15 pm.

This time we are to work with a limited color scheme of a land=scape of your own choosing.

Any one wishing to paint will be welcomed.

03.06.1962

g Progress
ulding Democrat and Paulding Co. Republican

PAULDING, OHIO, THURSDAY, MAY 31, 1962

2 From Paulding Win As Van Wert Art Show Opens

Judges for the sixth annual art show at Wassenberg Art Center, Van Wert picked 110 pictures out of 166 entries.

The show will open June 3 for a showing from 5 to 9 p. m. and again June 9, 10, 16, 17, 23, 24 from 1 to 9 p. m.

George Kakis of Continental won the grand award of $75 for his oil painting "The Journey."

Six entries were placed in the next five places with $35 awards. Winners were Amy Harrod, Ft. Wayne, water color; John Ross, Ft. Wayne, water color; Katie Stahl, Rt. 3, Paulding; Rita Kavolts, Defiance, water color and Pat Victor, Van Wert, water color.

Awards of $25 were presented to five entries. They were Mrs. Frank Mounts, Rt. 4, Van Wert, oil; G Dean Sheihline, Wapakoneta, lithograph; Eldor Gafham, Napoleon, oil; Hazel McClain, Lima, oil; Hilda S. Stoner, Ft. Wayne.

A special award the Lew Miller award was given to Pauline Link of Fayette, Ohio.

Receiving honorable mention were S. D. Grogg, Rt. 1, Venedocia, oil; Ferneau White, Paulding, oil; Mrs. Davis Cable, Lima, oil; O. Bud Bayliff, Cridersville, silkscreen and William L. Turner, Lima, water color.

Paulding Ohio Thursday May 31 1962

2 From Paulding Win as Van Wert Art Show Opens

Judges for the sixth annual Art show at Wassenberg Art Center, Van Wert picked 110 pictures out of 166 entries.

The show will open June 3 for a showing from 5 to 9 pm and again June 9 10 16 17 23 24 from 1 to 9 pm.

George Kakis of Continental won the grand award of $75 for his oil painting "The Journey".

Six entries were placed in the next 5 places with $35 awards. Winners were Amy Harrod Ft Wayne water color; John Ross Ft Wayne water color; Katie Stahl Rt 3 Paudling; Rita Kavoits Defiance, water color; and Pat Victor Van Wert water color.

Awards of $25 were presented to five entries. They were Mrs Frank Mounts Rt 4 Van Wert oil; G Dean Sheinline Wapakoneta lithograph; Elder Gafham Napoleon oil; Hilda S Stoner Ft Wayne.

A special award the Lew Miller award was given to Pauline Link of Fayette Ohio.

Receiving honorable mention were SD Grogg Rt 1 Venedocia oil; Ferneau White Paulding oil; Mrs Davis Cable Lima oil; O Bud Bayliff Cridersville silkscreen, and William L Turner Lima water color.

Painting Exhibition Draws Much Attention

The painting exhibition, held in the old Kroger store building on Wednesday and Thursday of last week, attracted widespread attention. The show consisted of landscapes, still life, florals in oil, watercolor and pastels from 13 area artists. Exhibiting at the show were Verda Leatherman, Chester Thrasher, Oakwood; Elsie Zemmer, Harlan, Ind.; Marilyn Murphy, Hicksville; Gene Hughes, Antwerp; Edith Pritchard, Eileen Vance, Ferneau White, Gene Barnes, Kate Stahl, Barbara Zimmer, Violet Noneman, Edna Preston, Paulding. Above is Ferneau White with 3 of her prize winning paintings that were on display. At the top is a painting "Toledo from Front St." that won 3rd place at the Bryan Art Show. At the bottom is "Togetherness" that won honorable mention at Van Wert Show. The painting on the left "Patio Still Life" was also accepted for hanging at the Van Wert Show.
— Progress Photo

The painting exhibition help in the old Kroger store building on Wednesday and Thursday of last week, attracted widespread attention. The show consisted of landscapes, still lifes, florals in oil, watercolor and pastels from 13 area artists. Exhibiting at the show were Verda Leatherman, Chester Thrasher, Oakwood; Elsie Zimmer Harlan Ind; Marilyn Murphy Hicksville; Gene (Jean?) Hughes Antwerp; Edith Pritchard Eileen Vance, Ferneau White, Gene Barnes, Kate Stahl, Barbara Zimmer, Violet Noneman, Edna Preston, Paulding.

Above is Ferneau White with 3 of her prize winning paintings that were on display. At the top is a painting "Toledo from Front Street" that won 3rd place at the bryan Art Show. At the bottome is "Togetherness" that won honorable mention at the Van Wert Show. The painting on the left "Patio Still Life" was also accepted for hanging in the Van Wert Show.

08.02.1962

TOLEDO BLADE NEWSPAPER

THURSDAY, JULY 26, 1962

Arts, Flowers Call Tune In Paulding

MAJOR ANDRE'S tragedy, during the War of 1812, gave citizens of Paulding, O., cause to celebrate. It seems that the major, a British spy who negotiated with Benedict Arnold for the surrender of West Point, was captured by three Ohioans, John Paulding, Isaac Van Wart and David Williams.

When northwestern Ohio was divided into counties in 1820, the county of Paulding (along with those of Van Wert and Williams) took its name for the War of 1812 hero, and about 20 years later, the town followed suit.

This year's celebration of John Paulding Days began yesterday at 4 p.m. with the opening of the Arts and Flowers Show in the Straw Bldg. on the town square.

The Better Homes and Garden Club of Paulding put on the flower show and the Paulding Art Club displayed paintings in the same building.

The flower show, which featured 72 exhibit classes, was open by invitation to a number of clubs in northwestern Ohio, who form Region II of the Ohio Association of Garden Clubs.

Mrs. Willis Strabele was general chairman of the flower show and Mrs. Charles Stahl, president of the art club, directed the "arts" section of "Arts and Flowers," which closes tonight at 10.

The arrangements in the show were classed into artistic design divisions. Among the titles were painting, dancing, sculpture, music, basketry and culinary art.

Last spring, the garden club gave zinnia seeds to the fourth grade students in the Paulding Village Exempted School. A special section of the show was set aside for them yesterday so that they might display the blossoms and demonstrate the plant development they had witnessed.

Entries were judged yesterday by Mrs. E. Dane Simon of Lima, O., an accredited judge with the Ohio association.

According to Mrs. Orrin Bennett, who served on the show committee, carnivals, parades and sidewalk sales will keep Paulding citizens celebrating through Saturday.

EDNA PRESTON, MRS. STAHL, JEAN BARNES

MRS. CHARLES BUEHLER AND MRS. STRABELE

Reprinted with permission of The Blade, July 26, 1962.
Story by Blade writer: Author not tagged on this article/Photos- Blade Photos
Luann Sharp, Assistant Managing Editor
The Blade
March 6 2013

Return to Paulding Progress paper

07-25-1963

ART EXHIBITS AT JOHN PAULDING DAYS LAST WEEK

Viewing the art exhibits in the old Kroger building during John Paulding Days last week are, left to right: Mrs. Mary Schilb, Mrs. Richard Schilb, and Mrs. Verne Tussing, all of Antwerp, and Violet Noneman, Paulding, General Chairman of the art exhibit.

The photo they are looking at is one of the paintings exhibited by Chester Thrasher of Oakwood. The entire, double-front building, was filled with the work of local and area artists.

g Pro
ding Democrat and Pauldi
NG, OHIO, THURSDAY, OCEOBER 10, 1963

Paulding Art Ass'n To Meet

Paulding Art Association short business and policy meeting will be held Wed. Oct. 16 at 7:30 during the regular painting session which begins at 7 o'clock. Please come with ideas to increase our effectiveness, or pass along your ideas to some who will attend.

All persons who are the least bit interested in painting are invited and urged to attend this meeting. Place, Library basement.

Violet at Sylvania Ohio Exhibit. 1963

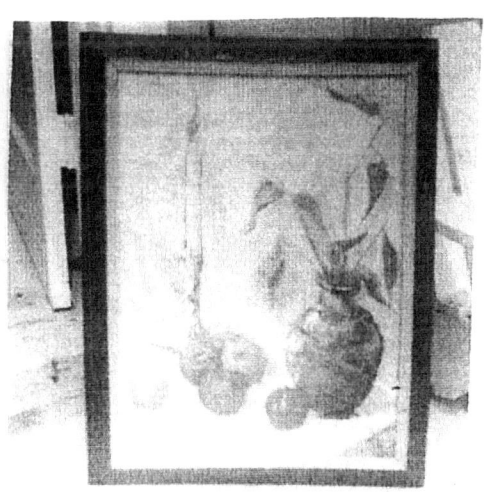

"CandleGlo"

Photos from Kerilyn Noneman Erne

Paulding Democrat and Paulding

PAULDING, OHIO, THURSDAY, APRIL 16, 1964

Artists To Hold Exhibit Apr. 25-May 9

The Paulding Artists Association is holding their spring exhibit at the Paulding County Library, April 25th to May 9th.

Exhibiters may bring three entries Thurs. April 23rd between 1:00 and 6:00 P. M.

The exhibit will open to the public at 2:00 P. M. Sat. April 25th with a coffee hour. The hours of the exhibit will be 1:00 to 8:00 P. M. daily except Saturdays when they are 1:00 to 5:00 P. M. The Library is closed on Sundays.

Paintings may be claimed Sat. May 9th between 3:00 and 4:30 P. M.

Mark these dates on your calender and plan to visit our show.

Paulding Democrat and Paulding

PAULDING, OHIO, THURSDAY, APRIL 23, 1964

Spring Art Exhibit Opens April 25th

The following members of the Paulding Art Association each had three painting hung in the recent Bryan Art Klan Exhibit, Isabelle Ringler, Elizabeth Paulus, Ferneau White, Martha McCague and Violet Noneman. One of Mrs. Noneman's paintings sold. Mrs. Paulus and Mrs. White each won Honorable Mention Jury Awards. Ferneau White also won the Popular vote award. This cash award is given each year for the painting chosen by the vote of the public as the painting they are most interested in.

These paintings may be seen at the Art Associations Spring Exhibit to be held at the Paulding Library April 25th to May 9th.

07-16-1964

Artists To Exhibit During John Paulding Days

5 Leaf Clover

If a 4-leaf clove brings good luck, think of the luck Dennis Sanderson 18, will have, as he found the above 5-leaf clover Tuesday, July 14th.

Dennis, son of Mr. and Mrs. Doyl Sanderson, Rt. 1, Paulding, found the clover along the driveway near their yard.

He is planning to have it sealed in plastic for safe-keeping.

"I'll Give You A Good Bang," Judge Tells Boy

"I'll give you a good bang," municipal Judge Robert L. Harrington of Van Wert told Thomas Lee Brown, 18, Grover Hill, when the youth appeared Thursday on charges of discharging firecrackers at the National Seal Corp. plant, where highly inflammable materials are manufactured.

The Judge assessed a fine of $50 a bang - $200 and costs - after the youth said, "I knew people who worked there and got a bang out of it," when asked why he discharged the four firecrackers.

Brown was arrested the evening of July 2 by city police. Juveniles involved in the incident will appear later in juvenile court.

Art Exhibit To Be Displayed In Former Kroger Store Building

The former Kroger building will be an attraction during John Paulding Days. Artists of Paulding County will show their work and visitors will be afforded an opportunity to spend eisurely hours viewing them.

The purpose of the show has been to encourage the artist to show his interpretations of local scenes and to stimulate the public to become interested in our efforts As one local artist suggested our slogan should be "Art for Everyone's Sake."

It is only by public interest and encouragement and our attempts to increase our standards of appreciation and performance that our community can show cultural growth. So bring your children and perhaps we can stimulate their interest in art.

Last year's show attracted thirty artists and nearly 900 registered for the painting which was given to the Lucky Art Viewer. Another painting will be given away this year.

This year any artist wishing to show his work may bring paintings Tuesday 1-4 p.m. July 21. An expense fee of $1.00 will be asked this year. We expect to be able to hang approximately 4 - 5 pictures of each entrant. Additional pictures may be entered if the entrant will supply table space. A hostess will be provided to care for sales.

Hours the exhibit will be open are 7 - 9 P.M. Wed., July 22, and 2 - 9 P.M. July 23, 24, and 25.

Be sure to enjoy our art exhibit when you enjoy John Paulding Days. We feel you'll be glad you came.

07-30-1964

ART EXHIBIT ATTRACTS LARGE CROWDS

The art exhibit in the Kroger store building, attracted large crowds during John Paulding Days. 15 artists exhibited their works of art with many having sale prices on their paintings. Artists in the show included; Mary Pat Marlin, Antwerp; Jean Hughes, Antwerp; Joan Dunlap, Oakwood; Martha McCague, Defiance; Kate Stahl, Peg Dotterer, Violet Noneman, Elizabeth Paulus, Wanda Webb, Nancy Stiger, Fern White, Eileen Vance, Edythe Pritchard, Wilma Miller and Isabel Ringler, all of Paulding. The painting on the easel on the left is by Wilma Miller; and at the right is a scene and painting of the scene by Joan Dunlap.

Over 1100 registered at the art show during the 4-day event. Gloria Andrews, Rt. 1, Oakwood, was the lucky winner of the painting that was given away.

Progress Photo

1965

Art Club 05-28-1965 Demonstration

Members of the Paulding Art Association are especially urged to attend next Tuesday meeting on May 25th.

Mrs. Nila Wallis has been rescheduled to give her painting demonstration at 7:30 sharp.

Please plan to be at the Library at 7:00 so you can be set up and prepared to paint along with Mrs. Wallis when she begins.

Notice - Art Club Members

Members please note change of meeting night from Tuesday to Wednesday at 7:00 P.M.

During last Tuesday's meeting a demonstration was given by Mrs. Nila Wallis. She did an oil painting of a vase of purple iris and wooden objects from a still life.

Members and guests present were Esther Corwin, Joy Deken, Peg Dotterer, Joyce Huseby, Bob Lindsay, Martha McCague, Wilma Miller, Elizabeth Paulus, Edythe Pritchard, Nancy Stiger, Myra Tow, Fern White, Sylvia Young, Millie Zur.

On Monday, May 31st Mrs. White, Mrs. McCague and daughter, Mrs. Dotterer, Mrs. Miller and Mrs. Huseby attended the Fine Arts Festival in Ft. Wayne where Mrs. White had paintings on display.

06-03-1965

Art Exhibition In Paulding During John Paulding Days

06-17-1965

This is to remind area artists that the Paulding Art Association has been invited to hold an exhibition in the Kroger Building during John Paulding Days, July 21-24. Why not plan to participate

We are making plans to paint outside on June 23 in the morning or afternoon. This will be discussed along with plans to visit the Van Wert Art Exhibition at Wassenberg Art Center, at our regular Wednesday night meeting, 7:00 P.M. in the Library basement.

Local Artists Work In Museum Show

11-04-1965

Ferneau White has been invited to participate in the Ft. Wayne Art Museums "Art For Sale," to be held Nov. 5, 6 and 7.

There is to be a display of Art objects, creations of Artists and Craftsmen from a hundred mile radius of the city. Every item will be for sale, and the entire museum will be turned over to the project. This will allow the public to make Christmas puchases from Articles more unique than can be found in Commercial shops. Stress will be put on quality at reasonable prices.

Mrs. White will show seventeen paintings including oils, monoprints and collages.

VOL. 16 NO. 38 01-15-1965

SIDEWALK
JOHN PA[ULDING]

Art Exhibit To Be Displayed In Kroger Building.

The former Kroger building will be an attraction during John Paulding Days. Artists of Paulding County will show their work and visitors will be afforded an opportunity to spend leisurely hours viewing them.

The purpose of the show has been to encourage the artist to show his interpretations of local scenes and to stimulate the public to become interested in our efforts. As one local artist suggested, our slogan should be "Art for Everyone's Sake".

It is only by public interest and encouragement and our attempts to increase our standards of appreciation and performance that our community can show cultural growth. So bring your children and perhaps we can stimulate their interest in art.

This year any artist wishing to show his work may bring paintings and hang them on Wednesday, July 21, 1-4 p.m. An expense fee of $1.00 will be asked this year. No expense fee will be collected from paid-up members of the Paulding Art Association. Entrants may hang any number of paintings provided there is enough space. A hostess will be provided to care for sales.

Hours the exhibit will be open are 7-9 p.m. Wednesday, July 21, and 2-9 p.m. July 22, 23, and 24.

Be sure to visit our Art Exhibit when you attend John Paulding Days. We feel you'll be glad you came.

ART CLUB NEWS 10-07-1965

Gusts present at the Wednesday night Art Club meeting, were: Carol Noneman, Jane White, Amanda Knisley, and Jackie Rike. New members are Ruby Humbarger and Jackie Thompson. Members present were: Wanda Webb, Peg Dotterer, Esther Corwin, Fern White, Joyce Huseby, Wilma Miller, Nancy Stiger, Micky Moore, and from Oakwood Joan Dunlap and Sylvia Young.

A recap of some of our Summer activities follows: On Monday August 30, a potluck dinner and outdoor painting session was held for the Paulding Art Club at the lovely home of Mrs. Martha McCague, Powell View Drive, Defiance. Those present were: Joan Dunlap and Verda Leatherman of Oakwood, Neva Clark and Florence Fruth of Holgate, Fern White, Wilma Miller, Wanda Webb, Nancy Stiger and Joyce Huseby all of Paulding.

During the Summer several members of the Paulding Art Club attended an evening class in oil painting and various techniques at the Defiance College, taught by Mr. John Nardker, a professor of art at Mount Saint Joseph-on-the Ohio College, St. Joseph, Ohio. Paulding members present were Joyce Huseby, Wilma Miller, Nancy Stiger, and Fern White, from Oakwood, Sylvia Young and Verda Martha McCague.

The Oakwood Art Show was held on Labor Day. Winners of the prizes were determined by popular vote, cast by visitors to the show. Fern White won first place with her landscape entitled "End of Summer." Third place went to Verda Leatherman who frequently joins us in our activities. And fourth place was won by Joan Dunlap another member.

PAINTINGS BY KATIE STAHL

ON DISPLAY AT 110 W. PERRY STREET

FINAL TWO WEEKS OF EXHIBIT

Select A Truly Meaningful Gift, For That Very Special Person, Which Will Continue To Increase In Enjoyment And Value.

OPEN SATURDAY FROM 2:00 P.M. THRU 6:00 P.M. DECEMBER 11th and 18th

For Appointment - Call: 399-5422

12-16-65

1966

THURSDAY, MARCH 17, 1966

Kate Stahl Memorial Exhibit Opened

A selected exhibit of the works of the late Kate Stahl, Paulding, opened Sunday, March 13. The exhibition consists of approximately 40 paintings in oil, watercolor, acrylic, collage and prints. The paintings are for sale except those on loan from private collections.

Kate Stahl was well-known in the art circles as a disciplined and sincere painter who experienced many techniques and media as may be viewed in this exhibit. Mrs. Stahl exhibited her works regularly and entered in many competitive exhibitions including Toledo, Ft. Wayne, Lima, Van Wert, and Florida. She received numerous awards for her painting, one of the latest being the award for abstract paintings in the national competition sponsored by the Mutual of New York Insurance Co. Many of these award winning paintings are in the present exhibit.

Mrs. Stahl shared her talents freely and was most helpful to other artists. She taught in the Paulding, and adult classes at the Wassenberg. She studied in Fort Wayne and Florida and belonged to the Ft. Wayne Artist Guild, and the Van Wert, Paulding, and Montpelier Art Clubs.

The exhibit will be open Saturday and Sunday, March 19 and 20th at the Wassenberg Art Center at Van Wert, Ohio. Other viewing times may be arranged by calling Isabel Drury, 233.0201, Van Wert. The exhibit is sponsored by the Van Wert Co. Art Club.

In relation to this exhibit on display will be four art books purchased for the Brumback Library as a memorial to Kate Stahl from the Ft. Wayne Artist Guild.

In addition to the memorial exhibit will be works by the Van Wert Co. Art Club in the South Gallery. In the lower gallery will be an exhibit of art works by students from the Starr Commonwealth Gordon Langley School. Examples of the various projects experienced throughout the year by grades 5 through 8 will be displayed. Included will be creative weaving, clay sculpture, paper mache masks, and collage. Mrs. Pat Victor is their instructor.

Art Exibit June 5th

The 10th annual Art Exhibition will open June 5 at the Wassenberg Art Center. The Prospectus is now available to artists of northwest Ohio and northeast Indiana. The exhibit is co-sponsored by the Van Wert County Art Club and the Van Wert County Foundation.

Entries will be received at the Art Center, May 21 and 22 from 2 to 9 p.m. An entry fee of $3 entitles the artist to submit three entries in any medium including painting, prints, drawings, ceramics and sculpture (50 pounds or under).

All paintings must be framed with watercolors and prints under glass. Screw eyes and wires must be attached to pictures. Sculpture must be assembled. All work will be handled and exhibited at the artists' risk. No mailed entries will be accepted.

The prospectus chairman reports artists in Dekalb and Noble counties in Indiana and Hardin and Hancock in Ohio are eligible for the first time.

Other eligible counties are Allen, Auglaize, Defiance, Fulton, Henry, Mercer, Paulding, Putnam, Van Wert and Williams in Ohio and Adams and Allen in Indiana.

The awards have also been increased to make allowance for the addition of ceramics and sculptures. A grand award of $75 will be given: six A awards of $35; six B awards of $25; the Lew Miller award of $25 for the best landscape in oil and six honorable mentions.

Further information may be obtained by contacting Mrs. Frank Argenbright, 302 W. Main Street, Van Wert, Ohio.

Serving on the jury for judging will be Otto G. Ocvirk, Professor of Fine Arts, Bowling Green State University, and Richard Wengenroth Associate Professor of Fine Arts, Ohio Wesleyan University, Delaware, Ohio.

THANKS 05-12-1966

To Show Paintings

Ferneau White will show thirty or more of her paintings at the Art Fair scheduled for June 11th.

The Ft. Wayne Artist Guild will hold its sixth Annual Art Fair in conjunction with the Indiana Sesquicentennial celebration at the "Landing" on the Columbia St. restoration, Ft. Wayne, Ind. from 8:30 till dark Saturday.

06-09-1966

PAULDING ART CLUB 09-22-1966
The Paulding Art Club is now meeting on Tuesday evenings at 7 o'clock below the library.

Paintings by Kate Stahl are being shown at 110 West Perry on every Friday from 4 to 8 P.M. or by appointment, by calling 399-5422. The paintings are for sale or may be rented. 50c1 10-14-1966

1967

PAULDING ART CLUB

The Paulding Art Club is meeting in the library on Tuesday evenings at 7:30 p.m. Those persons interested in painting are welcome to attend.

02-02-1967

THURSDAY, MAY 11, 1967

Rules For Art Exhibition Realeased

The prospectus is now available to resident artists of 16 northwest Ohio and northeast Indiana counties for the Eleventh Annual Art Exhibition opening June 4th. This exhibition is sponsored by the Van Wert County Art Club and is held at the Wassenberg Art Center, 643 S. Washington St., Van Wert, Ohio. Mrs. F. A. McCammon and her committee have mailed over 300 entry blanks to artists living in this area.

Entries will be received at the Wassenberg Art Center - May 20th and 21st from 2 to 9 p.m. An entry fee of $3.00 entitles the artist to submit three entries in any medium -- paintings, prints, drawings and ceramics or small sculpture (not to exceed 50 lbs.). All paintings must be framed, with watercolors and prints under glass. Sculpture must be assembled. Identification labels must be attached to the upper left-hand corner of back, screweyes and wires must be fastened to the pictures. All work will be handled and exhibited at the artist's risk. No mailed work will be accepted.

Artists eligible to exhibit must now be a resident of the following counties in Ohio: Allen, Auglaize, Defiance, Fulton, Henry, Mercer, Paulding, Putnam, Van Wert, Hardin, Hancock, and Williams. In Indiana: Adams, Allen, DeKalb, and Noble counties. Work must be original and must have been executed in the last two years, without the aid of a teacher. It should not have been shown in a former Van Wert June Exhibition.

The awards given are: Grand Award $75.00, six A awards, of $35.00, six B awards of $25.00, and six honorable mentions. The Van Wert County Foundation provides the funds for the above mentioned awards. The "Lew Miller Memorial Award" for outstanding landscape in any medium is an award of $25.00 and is given by Mr. L. C. Miller in memory of her husband.

The awards are given at the decision of a well qualified jury.

For further information or a prospectus, contact Mrs. F. A. McCammon, 141 Webster Ave., Van Wert, Ohio.

-p-p-s-

THURSDAY, JUNE 1, 1967 — PAULDING PROGRESS

Van Wert Annual Art Exhibit Judged

In Wednesday's judging of the 228 pieces of art submitted by 82 persons, in the 11th Annual Art Exhibit, Donald M. Glover and Raymond J. Fried selected 51 art objects to be exhibited.

There will be a reception for the artists and friends at the Wassenberg Art Center, Saturday evening, June 3rd from 8 to 10 p.m. when the awards will be presented.

Mr. Glover stated that he thought, "Van Wert will have a splendid show -- with a good number of beautiful things". Also that, "Persons who jury art exhibits look first for quality of artistic imagination".

In Mr. Fried's remarks he said, "It is a pleasant surprise to find such variety and high quality in the art work submitted for the Van Wert Art Exhibit and further stated that Van Wert is to be complimented for it's Cultural Benefactors and other interested people, for making an atmosphere in which talented people can produce".

Mr. Glover is the Curator for Education at the Dayton Art Institute and Mr. Fried teaches at the University of Toledo and the Toledo Museum of Art. They were a hard working and conscientious jury and worked the largest part of the day in selecting, the art work to be hung and the award winners.

List of award winners are:

GRAND AWARD

$75.00 - "Big Daddy" by Darvin Luginbuhl, Bluffton, Ohio, Ceramic

A AWARDS $35.00

"Trilogy", Acrylic, by Robert Johnson, Ft. Wayne, Ind.

"Unconformed Conformist", Wood and paint, by Margaret Whonsetler, Ft. Wayne, Ind.

"Language of Music", Oil, by Rena Trautman, Montpelier, O.

"Dixieland", Oil, by Ferneau White, Paulding, O.

"Summer Rhythm", Oil, by Russell Oettel, Ft. Wayne, Ind.

B AWARDS $25.00

"Landscape Forms", Watercolor by James McBride, Ft. Wayne.

"Mississippi River Bridge", Oil by Sam Grogg, Venedocia, O.

"Apples", Oil, by Maryanne Knapke, Celina, O.

"African Panel", Woodcut, by Martha Farmer, Lima, O.

"An Evening at Home", Woodcut, by Marjorie Heston, Edgerton, O.

LEW MILLER MEMORIAL $25.00

"Marshland", Watercolor Collage, by James Small, Napoleon.

HONORABLE MENTIONS

"Bridgeton Mill and Bridge", Woodcut, by P. W. Ashby, Kendallville, Ind.

"Herald of Spring", Oil, by Eldor Gathman, Napoleon, O.

"Ebling Woods", Watercolor, by James Strong, Lima, O.

"Mid Summer Night's Dream", Oil, by Lois Pieper, Ft. Wayne.

"Calvin", Needlepoint Print, by R. Lepo, Lima, O.

SPECIAL PURCHASE AWARDS

"Mississippi River Bridge", Oil, by Sam Grogg, Venedocia, O.

"Results of a Walk", Watercolor, by Dortha Cully, Van Wert, O.

"Blue Mountain" Watercolor, by Kathryn Mounts, Van Wert, O.

-p-p-s-

08-31-1967

Labor Day Art Show at Oakwood

The 12th Annual Labor Day Art Show will be held on the school lawn at Oakwood, O. on Monday, September 4th. Entries should be made between the hours of 8:30 and 10:30 on Labor Day, and prizes and ribbons will be awarded by 2:00 p.m.

Any amount of work may be entered, in any medium, but only original work will be judged. There will be a First, Second, Third, and Fourth prize and one prize that will be determined by spectator voting, to the most popular picture in the show. The entry fee is $3.00.

An added attraction this year will be the presence of Mr. Melvin Hubbard, an outstanding portrait artist from Lima, Ohio, who will be doing his work on the grounds.

everyone welcome.

J. Dunlap
Chairman, Art Committee

09-14-1967

Art Show Winners

Winners of the 12th Annual Labor Day Art Show in Oakwood, Ohio, have been announced. First prize was awarded to Fern White, Paulding; Second, Verda Leatherman, Oakwood, Third, Elizabeth Paulus, Paulding, and Fourth to Dorothy Argenbright of Van Wert. Honorable mention ribbons went to La Ree D. Little, of Cairo, Doris Greenwalt, Paulding, and Fern White. Most popular Picture in the Show award went to Douglas Miley, of Continental.

There were 14 artists exhibiting approximately 150 pieces, consisting primarily of oil paintings, but also including water colors, ceramics, prints, pencil sketches, a collage, and an interesting exhibition of custom-made tavern signs.

The weather was perfect for the annual out-door, one-day show, and crowds of people turned out to view, enjoy, and vote for their favorite display.

-p-p-s-

1968~1969

05-02-1968
Local Art Awards

Two members of the Paulding Art Association received awards at the Bryan Art Klan 9th Annual Exhibit. The show ended Sunday, April 18th with a tea given for the pleasure of Artists and friends.

The Grand Award of thirty five dollars went to Ferneau White for her oil painting "Still Life With Sun Flowers." An Honorable Mention went to Elizabeth Paulus for her painting titled "Onions."

There were one hundred and thirty-eight paintings in the exhibit. Judges for the show were: Dr. Paul Running, Professor of Art, Bowling Green University, and Mr. Harold Hasseltschwert, Art Instructor, Bowling Green University, Bowling Green, Ohio.

06-13-68
Boulevard Of Color

Two Paulding Artists, Ferneau White and Elizabeth Paulus, will participate in the Art Exhibition, June 13 through June 15, when the Ft. Wayne Artists Guild presents it's annual exhibition and sale in the Glenbrook Shopping Center, Ft. Wayne.

A juried Art Show will be held in the auditorium. The booth sales will be in the mall, with each artist manning his display.

The affair is open to professional resident artists of Indiana and Western Ohio. 51 artists will exhibit their work and be giving demonstrations for the public.

The Glenbrook Merchants Association will provide cash awards in the juried show.

Van Wert County Art Club 05-09-68
PROSPECTUS SENT FOR 12TH EXHIBIT

The twelfth annual art exhibit, sponsored by The Van Wert County Art Club, will open Sunday June 2nd, 1968 at the Wassenberg Art Center, 643 S. Washington Street, Van Wert, Ohio. The Prospectus is now available to resident artists of sixteen Northwest Ohio and Northeast Indiana Counties. Mrs. K. A. Pancake, Prospectus Chairman, and Mrs. F. A. McCammon, serving on the Committee, have mailed about 300 entry blanks to artists living in this area.

Entries will be received at the Wassenberg Art Center from 2 to 9 p.m. Saturday, May 18th and Sunday, May 19th, 1968. An entry fee of $3.00 entitles the artist to submit three entries in any medium - paintings, prints, drawings, ceramics or small sculpture (50 lbs. or less). All paintings must be framed, with watercolors and prints under glass. Sculpture must be assembled. Identification labels must be attached to the left corner of back of pictures and screw eyes and wires on the pictures. All work will be handled with utmost care, but will be received and exhibited at the artists' risk. No mailed work will be accepted.

Persons eligible to exhibit must now be a resident of the following counties in Ohio - Allen, Auglaize, Defiance, Fulton, Henry, Mercer, Paulding, Putnam, Van Wert, Hardin, Hancock and Williams. In Indiana - Adams, Allen, Dekalb and Noble. Work must be original and must have been done in the last two years, and not shown in any previous Van Wert Art Exhibition. Student work, or work done under the supervision of an instructor is not eligible.

The Van Wert County Foundation provides the awards listed below from funds left for this purpose by Mr. C. F. Wassenberg.

Grand Award, $75.00. Six "A" Awards, $35.00. Six "B" Awards $25.00, and Six Honorable Mentions. Also the Lew Miller Memorial Award for an outstanding landscape in any medium is given by Mrs. Lew Miller. Awards are given at the decision of a well qualified jury.

For further information or a Prospectus, contact the Chairman, Mrs. K. A. Pancake, 127 North Cherry St., Convoy, Ohio.

The Committee mailed Prospectus to the following colleges - Bluffton, Defiance, Saint Francis, Findlay, Fort Wayne Art School and Ohio Northern, and to the Art Clubs listed - Saint Marys, Defiance, Delta, Grover Hill, Paulding, Montpelier, Bryan, Celina, Lima, Fort Wayne and The Van Wert Art Club members.

04-10-1969
Art Exhibit

Ft. Wayne Artist Guild Show at the Woman's Club Gallery 402 W. Wayne will feature work that best represents the Guild Artists.

Ferneau White, Paulding, will have two oils in the show. The exhibit will be a large one with seventy members submiting work in oils, water color, collages and stichery.

The exhibit may be viewed by the public any time during April from 9 a.m. to 5 p.m.

The Interviews

All participants were asked the same questions, as follows:

How did you become interested in painting?
What was your most life defining moment?
What do you hope others remember about you?
What would be the most important thing you would want the world to know?

A OUR MOMMIES WOULD GO PAINTING TOGETHER

Mary Ruth Clark interviewed 10.27.2010

✽ **Interest in painting** : Mary Ruth shared with me that she became interested in painting because my mom Edythe talked her into lessens under Dr Edna Preston. She recalls painting lessons being conducted above an insurance company on Perry St for a spell. She had several children at the time and she fondly recalled that her son Mike decided to make some added touches to one of her paintings that was sitting on the dryer at her Miller Parkway home. She chuckled as she shared this; it was obvious she got a kick out of it. She loved the oil medium as she could easily correct anything she created. She stated that after Ed passed, she took tole painting up via lessons in Bryan Ohio.

✽ **Mary Ruth's most defining moment** in her life was when she lost her daughter Melanie. She said she simply did not want to go on. Her older daughters Kathie and Connie eventually came to her, sharing that they truly knew she was suffering. They continued that she still had children who needed her ….and this assisted Mary Ruth in coming back to life. She appreciates all of her children and considers herself blessed.

✽ **She hopes that others remember her** as a good mother, and most importantly that her life showed her children meant the world to her. She added lastly she hopes others remember that she was happy and she has a good, good life. Mary Ruth has continually demonstrated a gracious spirit. ✝

✽ **The most important thing she wants the world to know** is that there is hope, that peace can be real between nations and men in the future. Never give up hope.

◆ I had always been curious about how Ed got his nickname of Flop. Mary Ruth shared that during a football game Ed got the ball and began running to the wrong end zone. I guess his pals wanted to make sure he never forgot his flop. She continued to share more about Ed. Regarding him, Mary Ruth went on to share that upon Ed's return from the service, he attended church each and every week. Mary Ruth admitted that she was not that keen on attending everyyyy week ~ they were young, she said ~ when most do not equate attendance as a necessity at this stage of life. It was known he had a strong faith, Mary Ruth continued. Ed had promised God that if he returned home to the states, he would never miss church. And he kept his word. When he shared about his promise to God, she was taken by his commitment and his promise~ that was certainly made and kept throughout his life. This appeared to contribute to their strong marriage as well. ✝

Isabelle Ringler interviewed 11.16.2010

⌘ **Interest in painting:** Isabelle confessed that she was constantly drawing all her life. She shared that over tea (imagine that!) my mom encouraged her to get into painting. Isabelle said that Mom would encourage her even when it was a failure creation. (They likely were better that what Isabelle thought.) She had lessons under Fern White, Dr Preston and John Narkter (google him*) as well. She said they often painted in Dorothy Chester's garage. Under Dr Preston she learned water color, which was not truly a medium she liked. (She has an excellent water color of the Sugar Beat Factory and was done at the same angle that Mom did hers in oil…!) She said that they also would run to Oakwood to paint under a Joan Dunlap. Often she and Mom would go to Van Wert to the Olemdinger store in order to buy more oil paints. Isabelle cheered that her favorite medium was oil as she found them easier and also workable to adjust any mistakes or frustrations. Well, it turns out the Dr Edythe also "talked" Isabelle into entering the art shows in the Wassenberg Art Center in Van Wert Ohio, which is still open today. She entered into shows in Bryan Ohio as well.

⌘ **Isabelle's most defining moment** in her life was through her job as an LPN at the local hospital. She found the work very satisfying. In her attentiveness to her patients, she was able to show kindness and demonstrate the Good Book to others. ✞ She added that the actual "hands on" with the patients was much more educating than the text book of nursing. She added that if it was only 5 to 10 minutes of her time, she was personally obligated to be attentive and demonstrate God through her. By doing so consistently, they would truly never forget. She was convicted by her faith to do so and hoped that this commission of hers would spread by others sharing it forward. ✞

⌘ **She hopes that others remember her** as a loving person. She said that she loves all of her family and all of her grandchildren. She hurts when there are problems that she cannot help or cannot find the answers needed. She said she turns her concerns over to God. She loves regardless of what is going on personally or in the world. She said she is still compelled to assist others (likely the LPN in her). Her health has gotten in her way and~ she shared that if she is only able to make phone calls to cheer others on or up, then that is what she does. Isabelle has always been a gracious woman and I still delight in her little giggle that she has not lost. ✞

⌘ **The most important thing she wants the world to know** is that she is a Christian, a HAPPY mom, grandmother and great grandmother. She is proud of her children, grandchildren and great grandchildren. She confessed she wished she had a magic wand to establish lasting peace for all over this world. ✞

Eileen Vance Jeffery interviewed 11.17.2010

✶ **Interest in painting:** Eileen stated that she had been worked for 8-9 yrs and was used to doing something. With Mark being a new baby, she noted an ad in the Paulding Progress where Fern White was offering lessons in the basement of the library. She recalls that even as a child she wished she could paint. In her childhood, water colors were an only option. The classes at the library were her opportunity. So........she signed up and attended. With her new ability she painted with oil, because it is adjustable, if she had not reached the creation intended. Eileen studied under John Narkter as well (google him !).

✶ **Eileen's most defining moment** was when she married Bob. She said she was pre engaged to another at the time. Her cousin introduced them and when their eyes met, they simply KNEW they were it for each other. O youth.............!

✶ **She hopes that others remember her** as simply being a true nice person. She explained that everyone knows of her abilities with the piano. And she has had fun with this ability. She added that she played on stage in Florida with Dino once and it was quite exciting. However, nothing compares to what is inside of her, she share. In my words, not Eileen's, I would tag that as being kindness and joy. I have been witness to her life and she has consistently been a gracious lady.

✶ **The most important thing she wants the world to know** is to be kind to neighbors and keep peace within the communities. It starts at home. ✞

Elizabeth Paulus interviewed 06.17.2012

✤ **Interest in painting:** Elizabeth shared that she was always interested in art from grade school on. She started painting with a group of ladies who all were in the Paulding Art Club that met in the basement of the library. This group was partially composed of Ada Geyer, Merium Bickhard, Ann Arnold and Violet Noneman Robinson. Elizabeth's favorite medium is oil. She honestly did not know why oil, only that she always chose that over water color. I was able to photograph a favorite painting of mine, the blackberries. I remember distinctly of seeing this in an art show I believe was in our church basement (First Christian Church).

✤ **Elizabeth's most defining moment** was… **moments** throughout her life. She shared that she remembers each family move which included 5 different homes before the age of 18 yrs, which then included 9 different schools. She graduated from high school in Arizona. Her parents moved to Paulding and this is where she has lived the longest. She considers her life to be dull, simple. I see a woman who has done well, with life, health and family. She definitely has a sharp eye and ability when it comes to transferring God's creations onto a canvas.

✤ **She hopes that others remember her** as truly a good person and a friend.

✤ **The most important thing she wants the world to know:** surprised her when I asked. She laughed me off saying that is simply too hard to say for the length of time she has lived on this earth.

✞

* Photo reprinted with permission from the Toledo Blade newspaper, Luann Sharp, Editor March 12, 2013

✠ Fern White / Greg White, grandson interviewed 04.18.2012

I was able to stop by Greg White's home after work one day to snap some extra pictures of his grandmother's paintings. During this time, Greg shared that what he remembers most about her is that she had a real appreciation for painting, oil and water color both. She <u>really</u> enjoyed being around other artists and was most active in the Fort Wayne Indiana Art Guild. His grandmother was a school teacher, having graduated from the Bowling Green Teacher's College, as it was called in that day. She taught at the school on SR 500 and Co Rd 87, Paulding. It is obvious to him that her favorite medium was oil, and favorite subjects were landscapes and still life. When asked what he thought her most defining life event was he identified simply time around her husband, sisters, & family, and definitely teaching art.

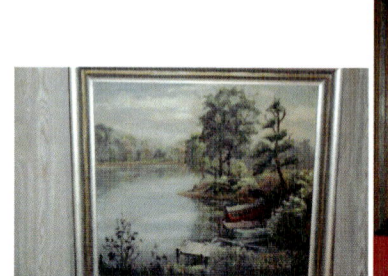

✠ Dr Edythe C Pritchard MD /sons Dr Kirkwood A Pritchard Jr PhD and Dr James C Pritchard MD

I wanted to complete information on my mother but did not want to do via myself, as I am authoring this project/book. So I decided to call upon my brothers.
(On 10.24.2012) Dr Kirkwood A Pritchard Jr PhD and (on 10.28.2012) Dr James C Pritchard MD provided the following thoughts/answers.

✠ **Interest in painting: Kirk** shared that he believed Mom simply always liked painting, tried it, and was good at it. He considers that she was friends with Dr Preston and Katie Stahl and they had an influence as well. **James** shared that Mom always had it in her. As a child, she loved all things on the earth. In her childhood she would have collected butterflies, etc. She learned to sew and create. She saw the world differently coming from her farm background. Everything was a jewel to her. She had great friends and great influences from others such as Dr Preston, Kate Stahl, and John Narkter. When she painted she found a depth that the average person would not have seen. James added it was shared to him that all of the ladies complained that they spent more time loading and unloading, than time in actual lessons. James added Mom was able to release us children to the backyard. She supervised us via the kitchen window, while painting on the stove which acted as her easel ~ of all things!

✽ **Mom's most defining moment : Kirk** shared that he felt Mom's decision to return to OSU to work in the child psychology unit in the late 70"s was her moment. Kirk recalls that he was in graduate school by then. He shared that Mom stood up to a superior there, in writing a script for an antibiotic for one of her patients. Her superior was insisting on protocol in that their unit was not to prescribe antibiotics. It would have to be done via another department. Mom indicated the ridiculousness of it as the goal for patients was to assist them to gain a healthy state. **James** said that he believes her moment was the death of her first husband. He pointed out that this stage of life was all new beginnings, and it was short lived, only 6 weeks with Airman Clyde Kaffenberger. She saw the plane crash and she knew it was his plane. While she sought refuge by going to bed for 6 weeks, upon arising again she was encouraged by her advisor that she needed to return to school for medicine. Women simply were not entering medicine in this time span! She was one of the first with other women as a result. **l/al!ce** would add the following. Mom often times would tear up, reveling in the beauty of the earth. Each time she would say she *simply could not* see how anyone would or could leave this earth due to its stunning beauty. I always thought this went back to her roots when she truly did farm labor. There she learned the values that she placed on all creation. I cannot recall which of her hospital stays preempted her sharing an event to me. One of her near deaths crossed her over to Heaven and back. From that time on, she no longer teared up about leaving this beautiful earth. There was no doubt in my mind that she had seen what was promised to us all.

✽ **She hopes that others remember her: Kirk** pointed out that Mom loved her husband and her kids over anything else in life. She loved everybody and life itself. She and Dad had an excellent relationship. Commitments made were done so in good faith and were kept. She was a strong advocate for what was right. **James** stated that there were so many things to list. The bulk of her life was built on loving life. There was nothing that did not fascinate her, whether it was sewing a dress one way different from the pattern, to working a garden, shaping clay, to painting, to plants overall, to science. She was raised in the depression era and had to hold onto things in print ~ *both* she and Dad were this way. She also could not say no to anything put in front of her. She was very community oriented and responsible as well. ✞ In sum, these may not be the memories Mom would have pointed out. They are, however, what we all recall about her.

✽ **The most important thing she would want the world to know : Kirk** first laughed saying that politics do not matter as much as family does. He summed that one should not take oneself too seriously and to enjoy life; enjoy what God has given ~ because it can quickly be gone. **James** indicated that this question matches what he shared above. He shared that her message was to love life ~~ don't waste it. There is a limited time on earth; appreciate the whole of what is around oneself. Love, art, life and God would have been her motto. And I concur with my brothers' comments. ✞

B Our Daddies, the men folk contributing to the delinquency of art and lessons on life, faith, and God's beauty

✎ **Gene Scarbrough interviewed 11.14.2012**
For as long as I have known Gene I never truly knew how he & Nova and Mom met. He shared that they met while doctoring with my parents. Because of the mutual love for art, they connected.
⌘ **Interest in art :**   Gene shared that drawing always came easy to him and he assumed that everyone could draw. Now at this time, school did not offer art. He was not good at reading, writing and arithmetic. Gene stated that he was bored in school and would rather draw, *which* he did, *which* lead him into trouble, *which* almost got him sent off to reform school…*which* did not happen! Upon graduating, he joined the Navy at age 18 years. While serving on a ship, the ship's paper needed an artist. He was the only one on board who drew. The ship's priest came to him regarding this task and Gene agreed. He and the priest developed a repertoire and bond during this time. These two remained lifelong friends. He left the Navy in 1946. Forty years later one of his Navy comrades called him saying that he needed a picture of Dale Earnhardt Snr ~ wanting Gene to do the work. Gene admitted that he had not followed racing so knew nothing of Dale Snr. Well, Gene did the drawing and it opened a "can of worms", according to him. Word got out about his skills. As his artful life progressed, the county commissioners asked Gene to paint murals in the main hall of the new fairground office building. His favorite medium is strictly pencil, because he confessed he is lazy. He laughed saying that with any other medium there is mess and clean up. I made sure my daughter Susanne met Gene ~ as she too had mastered pencil drawing as a child. It should be noted that Gene also did many community members' portraits for the *Bubba J's Buckeye* Café *on West Perry St in Paulding Oh. The restaurant hosted* the gallery of portraits *before it was bought by another Pauldingite proprietor.* Families were able to claim theirs to take home. All were grand works of art.
⌘ **Gene's most defining moment** has been *throughout* his life. He explained that he has truly had continuous 88 years of excitement. He claims he never "worked" a day in his life because he has enjoyed every minute of what he has done. He admitted that over the years he has taught art in the area, and began & still continues to do motivational speaking. This day he had just shared a motivational speech to local veterans, as we celebrate that November holiday for their works and protection of us all. ☏
⌘ **He hopes that others remember him** as one who truly loves his hometown and country. He said he has been all over the USA and nothing compares to his Grover Hill. It is his Garden of Eden. He hopes that everyone learns to shape their outlook on life~ in that it is all balanced by one's perspective, beliefs, and approach to everything. He shared it is *all* in the thinking! If one thinks good thoughts, good things happen. If one thinks bad things, bad things happen. He is not discounting the realities of life and events. These realities can be defeating or *by turning the negative around*, it becomes a positive which does not hold one captive. (Footnote: This takes practice; so keep up the good!)
⌘ **The most important thing he wants the world to know:** is what he just shared above. He emphasized that if one's thinking is sincere, wholesome, and positive, one will not be sick; one will see the world differently with all things being good. If one wants to master something like drawing, think, study and begin; it will happen. The power is truly within us.

🖎 🖎 🖎 🖎 🖎

🖎 **John Narkter** : Regarding this amazing man and friend of my mom, one must simply check out the information via the web. His bio is listed as well as his works. I would suggest this link :
http://www.nartkerstudio.com/index.html
On the left hand side one can choose **Artist's Other Works** which will provide the following **Paintings/ Ceramics/ Prints.**
My brother James met Mr Nartker in Cincinnati. Mr Nartker asked him if he happened to know Edythe Pritchard to which James replied, "Yes she is my mother." Small world, eh?

🖎 🖎 🖎 🖎 🖎

🖎 **H G Davisson:** of Fort Wayne Indiana became a friend to my mom as well. The easiest link I could find on him was through: **Fort Wayne** Observed: **Davisson** artwork sold
indiana.typepad.com/fwob/2007/12/**davisson**-**art**wor.html
Homer G. **Davisson** (1866-1957) was an Indiana artist and art teacher in a couple different schools. I have three of his paintings in my collection. One may recall seeing them in my parents' office. I value the eye he had. They are all places I wish I could walk in the world he captured on canvas! The ones I own are below!

 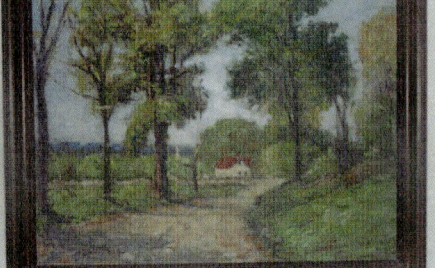 

The Eulogy Tributes

This book would be incomplete if we did not celebrate those Stars who have passed over to Heaven.

The Progress grants permission to Alice Gerber to reprint obituaries and any other published material regarding the Art Study Club that was published in the Paulding Progress or the Payne Reflector, Melinda Krick, Editor   March 11, 2013.

1965 (_____ to June 1, 1965) Catherine (Katie) Stahl

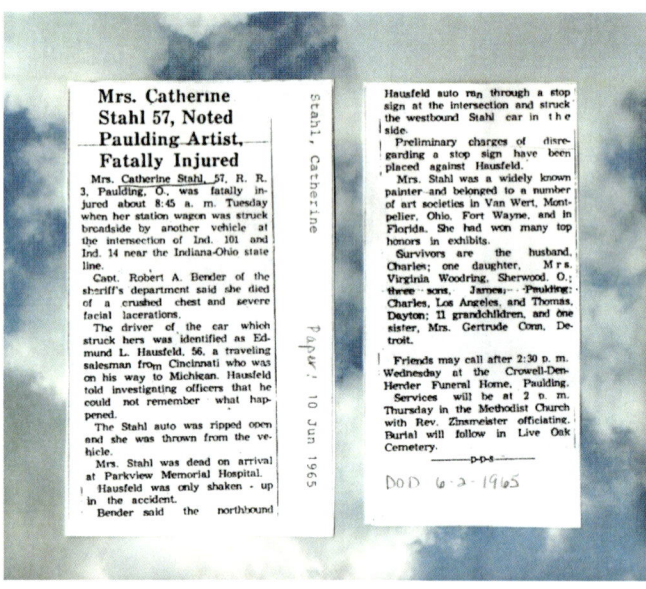

EDNA PRESTON, MRS. STAHL, JEAN BARNES
...at Arts and Flowers show in Paulding *

Photo reprinted with permission from the Toledo Blade newspaper, Luann Sharp, Editor March 12, 2013

1966 (July 3 1914 to August 31, 1966) John H Peeper

John H. Peeper *1966*

John H. Peeper, 52, a former Paulding area teacher, died at 11:45 p.m. Wednesday at the Paulding County Hospital, where he had been a patient for nine days. *31 AUG.*

A native of Hicksville, he was born July 3, 1914, the son of Earl and Edith (Crouse) Peeper. He attended Bowling Green University and was a graduate of the Ringling School of Art at Sarasota, Fla. He was a veteran of World War II, a former member of the board of public affairs, an elder of the First Christian Church and sales representative of the Advance Glove Co. of Detroit, Mich.

Surviving are his widow, the former Sonia Velkoff; two daughters, Marilou and Melissa and a son John E., all at home; his mother, Mrs. Edith Carr of Paulding; two sisters, Mrs. Maxine Boundy of Paulding and Mrs. Earline Clark of Fort Wayne.

Services were conducted at 2:00 p.m. Saturday at the First Christian Church of Paulding with the Rev. Hal Zug officiating. Interment in Live Oak Cemetery, Paulding.

Peeper, John H.   31 Aug 1966

1994 (March 5, 1882 to January 17, 1994) Dr Edna Preston

DR EDNA PRESTON

PAULDING — Dr Edna Layman Preston, 91, 342 S Main St, died at 7:15 pm Jan 17 in the Paulding County Hospital, where she had been a patient 10 hours.

A native of Reed City, Mich, she was born there March 5, 1882 to Alfred and Elnora (Bone) Flarida. She was a graduate of Ypsilanti State Normal College, Columbia University in New York and the Ohio College of Chiropody.

She taught art 20 years in public schools and colleges in Michigan, Oregon and Cleveland, and was a chiropodist in Defiance and Paulding from 1935 to 1972. Dr Preston was a member of the Paulding Presbyterian Church.

Surviving are a son, Virgil Layman, Defiance; eight grandchildren, 30 great-grandchildren and one great-great-grandchild. Her first husband, John Layman, died in 1930 and her second husband, Frank Preston, in 1950.

Services were held Sunday in the Presbyterian Church, Dr John Luchies officiating, and graveside services were held Monday in Woodlawn Cemetery, Reed City, Mich. Crowell-DenHerder Funeral Home was in charge of arrangements.

Preston, Edna Layman 23 Jan 1994

1975 (December 2. 1908 to July 12, 1975)   Carl E Chester

Carl E Chester went home to his Lord on July 12,1975. He was born in Paulding County to Don and Elizabeth Chester. He grew up with 2 sisters and 3 brothers. He graduated from Paulding High School in 1928. Carl was employed by the Nickel Plate Railroad Company, and working in the towns of Latty and Payne Ohio. He married Dorothy (Stores) on April 12, 1930. They had two daughters Mary Jane (John) Englehart and Rowena (William) Bashore, both of Paulding. He took up painting in the late 1960's and completed several works of art for his family and his own joy. He also enjoyed gardening and playing cards in his spare time. He loved the Cleveland Indians!

Surviving are his wife Dorothy, two daughters and four grandchildren. Visitation was handled by Den Herder's Funeral Home. The Celebration of his life was held at St Paul's Lutheran Church with burial at St Paul's Cemetery, Paulding Ohio.

✝An obit on Carl could not be located in any county or neighboring newspapers. With the help of his family, we have
created one. His death certificate documents that he passed on the 12th of July

1992 (September 29, 1920 to June 2, 1992) Dr Kirkwood A Pritchard MD (Mom's biggest fan!)
1994 (October 2, 1918 to October 28, 1994) Dr Edythe C Pritchard MD

KIRKWOOD PRITCHARD, M.D.

PAULDING — Kirkwood A. Pritchard, M.D., 71, of 742 Miller Parkway Drive, died at 3:36 a.m. June 2 in Parkview Memorial Hospital, Fort Wayne, after an automobile-truck accident at 10:30 p.m. Monday at the intersection of U.S. 30 and Indiana 101.

Dr. Pritchard was born Sept. 29, 1920, in Cleveland, the son of Kirkwood A. and Victoria R. (Sims) Pritchard. On June 16, 1948, he married the former Edythe (Clay) Pritchard, M.D., who survives.

He entered the practice of general medicine and surgery in 1952 in Paulding and served the community for 40 years. He also was a member of the village council and served on term as mayor.

He was a graduate of Cathedral Latin School, Cleveland and attended both Westminster College and the University of Pittsburg while serving as a medical corpsman in the U.S. Army and the U.S. Coast Guard. He was a pre-med graduate of the University of Wyoming and graduate of Ohio State University School of Medicine in 1947. Dr. Pritchard interned in general medicine and was a resident in general surgery at St. Rita's Hospital, Lima. He was a member of St. Joseph Catholic Church, Paulding, and was a member of its choir.

Also surviving are two daughters, Mrs. Laura Gibson of Attica and Mrs. Ron (Alice) Gerber of Haviland; two sons, Kirkwood A. Pritchard Jr., Ph.D., of White Plains, N.Y. and James C. Pritchard, M.D., of Cincinnati; one sister, Mrs. Carolyn V. Tobin of Sidney, Neb.; one brother, Howard T. Pritchard of Kensington, Md.; and four grandchildren.

He was preceded in death by his parents, a sister, Suzanne Pritchard and brother, Robert Pritchard.

Funeral services were held Saturday at St. Joseph Catholic Church of Paulding with the Rev. Cleo S. Schmenk officiating. Burial was in St. Paul Cemetery, Paulding Township. DenHerder Funeral Home was in charge of arrangements.

Memorials may be made to Paulding County Memorial Hospital, the St. Joseph Indian School or the donor's choice.

DR. EDYTHE PRITCHARD

PAULDING — Dr. Edythe C. Pritchard, 76, Paulding, died at 11:50 a.m. Friday, Oct. 28, 1994, at Dallas Lamb Foundation Home, Payne.

She was born Oct. 2, 1918, in Seneca County, the daughter of Newton and Bertha (Myers) Clay. In 1948, she married Kirkwood Pritchard, who preceded her in death. A physician, she received her B.A. from Capital University in 1940, taught for one year and returned to school to receive her M.S. at Ohio State University and did further residency in child psychiatry in 1978-79. She specialized in internal medicine. She and her husband completed their internship in Lima at St. Rita's Hospital, and graduated with their MDs in June 1949. They moved to Paulding and established a medical practice in August 1951. The practice closed in 1992.

She was active in her earlier years as a school physician, the Paulding MRDD chapter, the Child Conservation League and a painting club consisting of Paulding's own artists. She assisted in gaining a youth center for Paulding. She served on the local and tri-county mental health boards, served as a Girl Scout and Cub Scout leader, served as a science fair judge and led Chi-Ro youth at the First Christian Church and was Woman of the Year in 1976. She was a member of the First Christian Church of Paulding, the local medical society, the Ohio State Medical Society, the American Medical Association and the Ohio State Teachers Association.

Surviving are two sons, Kirkwood A. Pritchard, Ph.D. of Brookfield, Wis., and James C. Pritchard, M.D. from Cincinnati; two daughters, Alice Gerber of Haviland and Laura Gibson of Attica, Ohio; and five grandchildren.

Also preceding her in death was a brother, Clifford Clay.

Services were Tuesday at the First Christian Church with the Rev. Dawn Remster officiating. Burial was in St. Paul Cemetery.

Preferred memorials are to the church, Paulding County Heart Association, Paulding County Cancer Society, Paulding County Home Health, Dallas Lamb Foundation Home, or Paulding County Visiting Nurses Association.

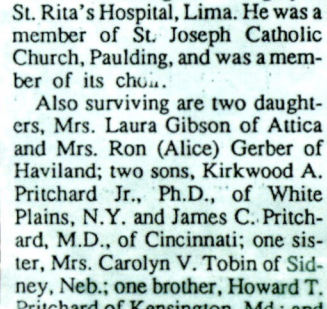

1998 (June 28, 1904 to March 9, 1998) Ferneau White

FERNEAU JUNE WHITE
1904-1998 *11 Mar*

PAULDING — Ferneau June White, 93, formerly of Fort Wayne, died Monday, March 9, at Ossian Health C__ in Ossian, Ind.

She was born June 28, 1904 in Paulding County, the daughter of Robert and Fann_ (Ferneau) Treece. In 1926, she married Ernest "Red" White, who preceded her in death in 1979. She was a homemaker and local artist and a 70-year member of the First Christian Church, Paulding.

Surviving are one daughter, Sally (John) Shriner of Fort Wayne; one son, John "Jack" White of Dundee, Mich.; 10 grandchildren; and 18 great-grandchildren.

Also preceding her in death were four sisters, Florence Wiegel, Edna Margaret VonKlinger, Olive Johnson, and Senna Veda Turner.

Services will be held at noon on March 12, in Den Herder Funeral Home, Paulding, with visitation beginning at 10 a.m., Rev. Dawn Remster will officiate at the services. Burial will be in Live Oak Cemetery, Paulding.

Preferred memorials are to The American Cancer Society.

White, Ferneau June Treece 11 Mar 1998

MR AND MRS ERNEST WHITE
Photo By Hodge

Observes Fiftieth Wedding Anniversary

2004 (June 17, 1925 to February 5, 2004) Genevieve Rife

GENEVIEVE RIFE
1925-2004

PAULDING — Genevieve R. Rife, 78, of Paulding, died at 6 a.m. Thursday, Feb. 5, at her residence.

She was born June 17, 1925, in Paulding County, the daughter of Charles F. and Rose (Carrier) Noneman. On Oct. 26, 1946, she married Albert Rife, who preceded her in death March 3, 2002. She was an assistant librarian for the Paulding Carnegie Library, retiring in 1994, following 25 years of service. She was a member of the St. Joseph's Catholic Church, Paulding, CLC of St. Joseph, VFW Post 587, Eagles Auxiliary 2405, and the American Legion of Continental.

Surviving are two sons, Roger (Nancy) Rife of Swanton and Jeffery (Cindy) Rife of Fort Wayne; two daughters, Alice (Mark) Fasman of St. Louis, and Barbara (Frederick) Koch of Paulding; a brother, James Noneman of Paulding; two sisters, Agnes Heimann of Paulding and Mildred Siebenick of Defiance; nine grandchildren; and two great-grandchildren.

Also preceding her in death were six brothers, Bill, Bernard, Frank, Ernest, Arthur and Charles Noneman; and two sisters, Leona Berg and Mary Dager.

Services were held on Saturday, Feb. 7, at St. Joseph's Catholic Church in Paulding, with the Rev. G. Allan Fillman officiating. Burial was in the Paulding Memorial Cemetery. Den Herder Funeral Home was in charge of the arrangements.

Preferred memorials are to the Masses or to Paulding County Area Visiting Nurses and Hospice.

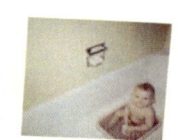

Rife Genevieve R   5 Feb 2004

2006 (September 12, 1908 to February 5, 2006) Dorothy Chester

DOROTHY CHESTER
1908-2006 8 Feb

PAULDING — Dorothy F. Chester, 97, died Sunday, Feb. 5, at the Dallas Lamb Foundation Home in Payne.

She was born Sept. 12, 1908, in Paulding County, the daughter of Albert W. and Mary (Yoder) Stores. On April 12, 1930, she married Carl E. Chester, who preceded her in death on July 15, 1975. She was employed at the Brune Printing Company, retiring in 1974. She was a graduate of Bowling Green State University. She was a former teacher at Payne Elementary School, and had been employed at the Paulding County Treasurer's office, and the former A.S.C. office of Paulding County. She was a former 4-H adviser for many years and was a genealogy enthusiast.

Surviving are two daughters, Mary Jane (John) Englehart and Rowena (William) Bashore, both of Paulding; four grandchildren; and eight great grandchildren.

Graveside services will be held at noon today, Feb. 8, at St. Paul Cemetery, Paulding, with Pastor Mary Beth Smith-Webb officiating.

Hours of visitation will be from 11 a.m.-noon today, at Den Herder Funeral Home, Paulding.

Preferred memorials are to the Dallas Lamb Activity Fund.

2004 (November 1, 1911 to September 6, 2006) Violet Robinson

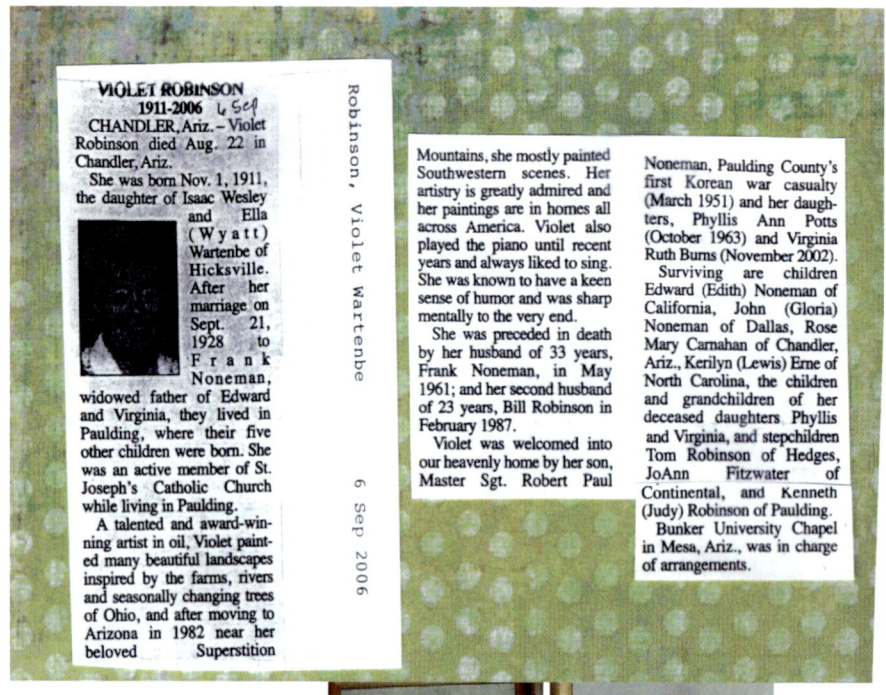

VIOLET ROBINSON
1911-2006 6 Sep

CHANDLER, Ariz. – Violet Robinson died Aug. 22 in Chandler, Ariz.

She was born Nov. 1, 1911, the daughter of Isaac Wesley and Ella (Wyatt) Wartenbe of Hicksville. After her marriage on Sept. 21, 1928 to Frank Noneman, widowed father of Edward and Virginia, they lived in Paulding, where their five other children were born. She was an active member of St. Joseph's Catholic Church while living in Paulding.

A talented and award-winning artist in oil, Violet painted many beautiful landscapes inspired by the farms, rivers and seasonally changing trees of Ohio, and after moving to Arizona in 1982 near her beloved Superstition Mountains, she mostly painted Southwestern scenes. Her artistry is greatly admired and her paintings are in homes all across America. Violet also played the piano until recent years and always liked to sing. She was known to have a keen sense of humor and was sharp mentally to the very end.

She was preceded in death by her husband of 33 years, Frank Noneman, in May 1961; and her second husband of 23 years, Bill Robinson in February 1987.

Violet was welcomed into our heavenly home by her son, Master Sgt. Robert Paul Noneman, Paulding County's first Korean war casualty (March 1951) and her daughters, Phyllis Ann Potts (October 1963) and Virginia Ruth Burns (November 2002).

Surviving are children Edward (Edith) Noneman of California, John (Gloria) Noneman of Dallas, Rose Mary Carnahan of Chandler, Ariz., Kerilyn (Lewis) Erne of North Carolina, the children and grandchildren of her deceased daughters Phyllis and Virginia, and stepchildren Tom Robinson of Hedges, JoAnn Fitzwater of Continental, and Kenneth (Judy) Robinson of Paulding.

Bunker University Chapel in Mesa, Ariz., was in charge of arrangements.

Robinson, Violet Wartenbe 6 Sep 2006

2010 (July 21, 1917 to April 26, 2010)   Sonya Velkoff Peeper

SONIA PEEPER
1917-2010

2 May

PAULDING – Sonia M. (Velkoff) Peeper, age 92, died Monday, April 26 at her home.

She was born July 21, 1917 in Chicago, the daughter of Matodi and Louise (Beck) Velkoff. The family moved to Fort Wayne, where Matodi opened St. Joseph Hospital radiology department. She attended Southside High School, graduating in 1936, and attended Parsons School of Art and Design in New York. Upon graduation in 1939, she came back to Fort Wayne where she met and married John H. Peeper of Paulding, who preceded her in death in 1966.

Upon his death, Sonia went back to school at Defiance College and earned her BA degree, cum laude. In 1970, she was hired as director of the Paulding County Welfare Department, retiring in 1985. She was an active member of many social service boards. She was instrumental in developing Paulding County Mental Health Agency to serve county residents. She opened Westside Stories, a paperback buy-sell-trade business in 1986. She operated her business until her health forced her retirement. She still actively continued to support her community through membership on many boards and committees until her health would no longer let her. She was a member of First Christian Church of Paulding.

Surviving are a son, John E. Peeper of Paulding; two daughters, Marilou Schrimshaw of Coppell, Texas and Melissa (John) Munger of Paulding; five grandchildren; and four great-grandchildren; and a brother, Dr. Cy Velkoff, of Warriors Mark, Pa.

She also was preceded in death by a brother, Henry R. "Hank" Velkoff.

Funeral services were held Saturday, May 1 at Den Herder Funeral Home, Paulding, with the Rev. Greg Bibler officiating. Burial was in Live Oak Cemetery, Paulding.

Preferred memorials are to Paulding County Dog Shelter or Community Health Professionals of Paulding and Hospice.

Online condolences may be sent to www.denherderfh.com

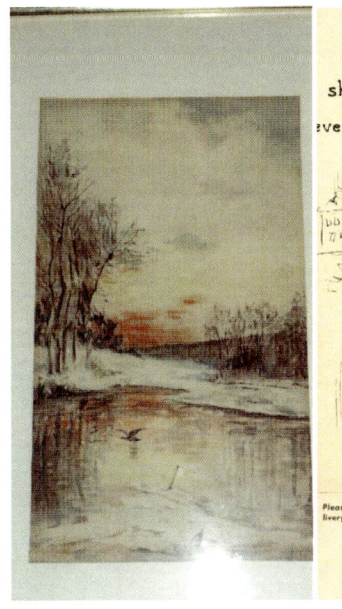

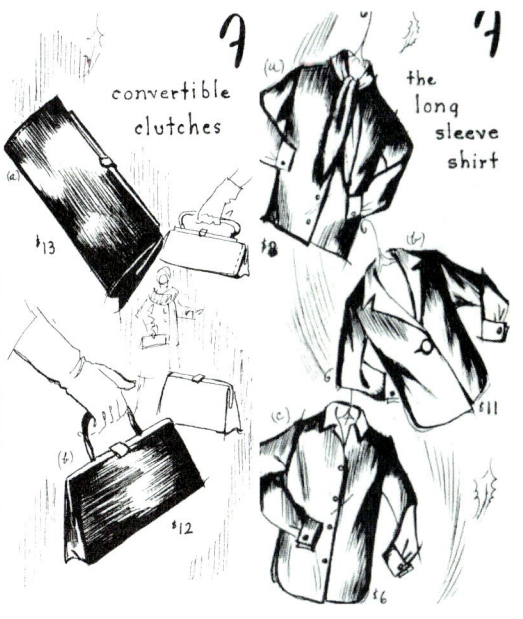

2012 (November 8, 1929 to October 1, 2012) Mary Ruth Clark

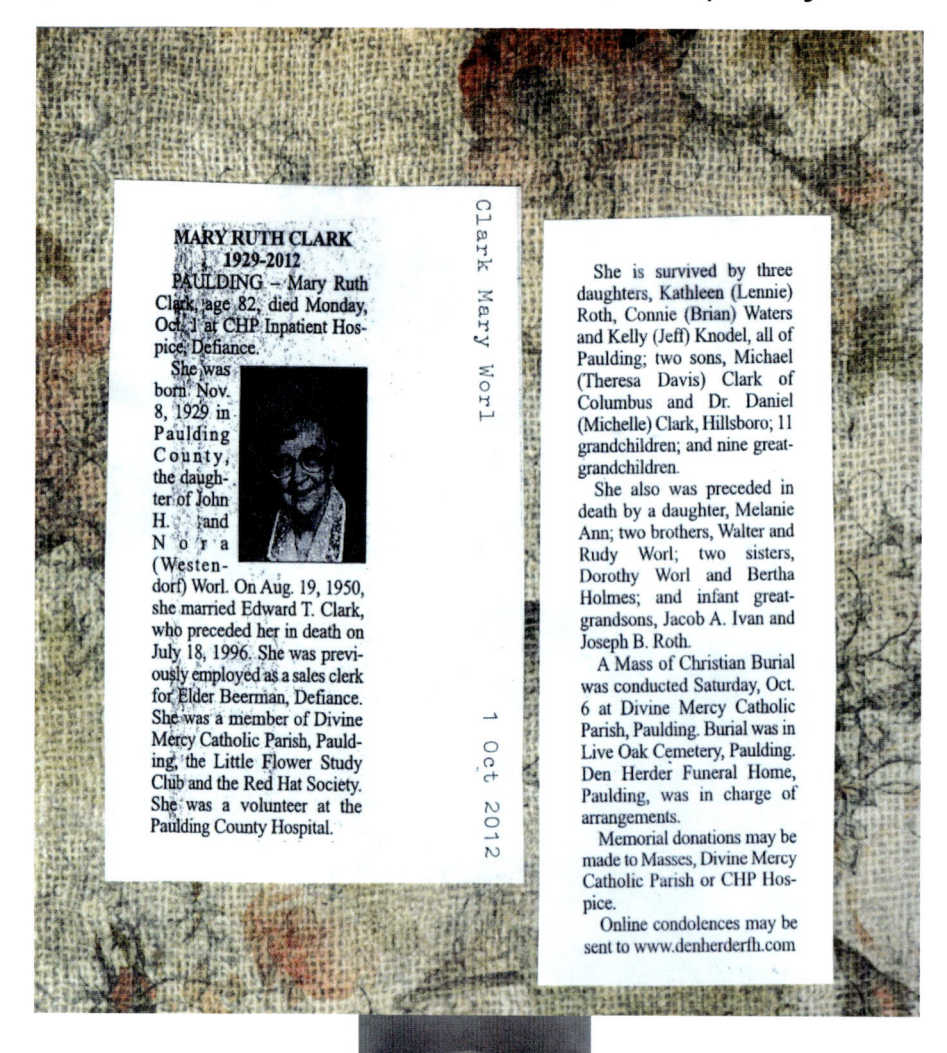

MARY RUTH CLARK
1929-2012

PAULDING — Mary Ruth Clark, age 82, died Monday, Oct. 1 at CHP Inpatient Hospice, Defiance.

She was born Nov. 8, 1929 in Paulding County, the daughter of John H. and Nora (Westendorf) Worl. On Aug. 19, 1950, she married Edward T. Clark, who preceded her in death on July 18, 1996. She was previously employed as a sales clerk for Elder Beerman, Defiance. She was a member of Divine Mercy Catholic Parish, Paulding, the Little Flower Study Club and the Red Hat Society. She was a volunteer at the Paulding County Hospital.

She is survived by three daughters, Kathleen (Lennie) Roth, Connie (Brian) Waters and Kelly (Jeff) Knodel, all of Paulding; two sons, Michael (Theresa Davis) Clark of Columbus and Dr. Daniel (Michelle) Clark, Hillsboro; 11 grandchildren; and nine great-grandchildren.

She also was preceded in death by a daughter, Melanie Ann; two brothers, Walter and Rudy Worl; two sisters, Dorothy Worl and Bertha Holmes; and infant great-grandsons, Jacob A. Ivan and Joseph B. Roth.

A Mass of Christian Burial was conducted Saturday, Oct. 6 at Divine Mercy Catholic Parish, Paulding. Burial was in Live Oak Cemetery, Paulding. Den Herder Funeral Home, Paulding, was in charge of arrangements.

Memorial donations may be made to Masses, Divine Mercy Catholic Parish or CHP Hospice.

Online condolences may be sent to www.denherderfh.com

Clark Mary Worl 1 Oct 2012

Epilogue

Yes all the mommies would go
painting together.
How they raised their brushes
and us
at the same time
speaks well of their souls . . . .

Their works enriched their lives and friendships,~ as well as ours, as their children and grandchildren. I pray this book has celebrated all of them, as well as their art. God bless our families always.

1 Thessalonians 5: 21
Make sure of all things and
hold fast to that which is fine.
✝ Amen ✝

Three little Edythes I see I see.
Audra Lynn Schoenauer was seen in this book standing next to Mom's roses.
Susanne Louise Gerber was seen in this book standing next to Dr Preston's roses.
Jack Edward Schoenauer is my clip art. He is a great grandson to Mom and Dad.

Kirk and Marilyn Pritchard's children
Sarah Victoria Pritchard is the second born.
Emily Morgan Pritchard is the 3rd born,
while Kathryn Grace (Kati) Pritchard is 1st born.

James and Siobhan Pritchard's children
Elizabeth Clare Pritchard
& Kathleen Anna Pritchard

Honorable mention: Mary Millen Waters

(My pretend production, press and foundation company)
SureFoot Productions SR637jNRd24
by
NewtonAndBerthaClayPress
In conjunction with
"Go Team Go" KAPECP Family Foundation

ONLY in Paulding County 063 OHIO

All Rights Reserved. Nothing in this book may be copied or reprinted without written permission by this author.

Now it is time for some hot tea!

Then kiss me good night!
God Bless!